A Beginners Guide to
Training in
Counselling & Psychotherapy

A Beginners Guide to Training in Counselling & Psychotherapy

Edited by
Robert Bor and Stephen Palmer

SAGE Publications
London • Thousand Oaks • New Delhi

First published 2002

SAGE Publications Ltd
6 Bonhill Street
London EC2A 4PU

SAGE Publications Inc
2455 Teller Road
Thousand Oaks, California 91320

SAGE Publications India Pvt Ltd
32, M-Block Market
Greater Kailash – I
New Delhi 110 048

British Library Cataloguing in Publication data

A catalogue record for this book is available
from the British Library

ISBN 0 7619 6429 0
ISBN 0 7619 6430 4(pbk)

Library of Congress Control Number:

Typeset by Mayhew Typesetting, Rhayader, Powys
Printed and bound in Great Britain by The Cromwell Press Ltd,
Trowbridge, Wiltshire

To all of the trainee therapists with whom I have had the pleasure to work
Robert Bor

To Pat Milner, a colleague, friend and mentor
Stephen Palmer

Contents

The Editors

ROBERT BOR

Robert Bor is Professor of Psychology at London Guildhall University and also Head of the HIV Counselling Unit at the Royal Free Hospital, London. He is a Chartered Clinical, Counselling, and Health Psychologist and is the Director of Counselling Psychology Courses at London Guildhall University. He trained in the practice and teaching of family therapy at the Tavistock Clinic, is a member of the Tavistock Society of Psychotherapists, a clinical member of the Institute of Family Therapy (London) and is a UKCP Registered Systemic Psychotherapist. He is also a member of the American Psychological Association, American Family Therapy Academy and American Association for Marital & Family Therapy.

His recent books include *The Trainee Handbook* (with Mary Watts, 1999), *Counselling in Health Care Settings* (with Miller, Latz & Salt, 1998) and *The Practice of Counselling in Primary Care* (with Damian McCann, 1999). He serves on the editorial board of a number of journals including *Counselling Psychology Quarterley*, *AIDS Care*, *British Journal of Guidance and Counselling*, *European Journal of Psychotherapy*, *Counselling and Health*, *Psychology, Health & Medicine* and *Families, Systems and Health*.

He is extensively involved in counselling training in the UK and abroad. He is also a qualified pilot and conducts research into passenger behaviour. He provides a specialist counselling service for air crew and their families. He received the British Psychological Society Division of Counselling Psychology Annual Counselling Psychology Award in 1997 for Outstanding Scientific Achievement. He is also a Churchill Fellow.

STEPHEN PALMER

Professor Stephen Palmer PhD is Director of the Centre for Stress Management, London, an Honorary Professor of Psychology in the

Centre for Health and Counselling Psychology at City University, and a Visiting Professor in the School of Lifelong Learning and Education at Middlesex University. He is Fellow of the British Association for Counselling and Psychotherapy, a Chartered Psychologist (Health & Counselling), UKCP registered psychotherapist, and a certified supervisor of Rational Emotional Behaviour Therapy.

He is editor of the *Rational Emotive Behaviour Therapist*, and the *International Journal of Health Promotion and Education*, and Co-editor of the Counselling Psychology section of the *British Journal of Medical Psychology*. He has written numerous articles on counselling and stress management and authored or edited over 20 books. Some of his recent books include *Handbook of Counselling* (with McMahon, BACP & Routledge, 1997), *Integrative Stress Counselling* (with Milner, Cassell, 1998). *Counselling in a Multicultural Society* (with Laungani, Sage, 1999), *Trauma and Post-traumatic Stress Disorder* (with Scott, Cassell, 2000), *Introduction to Counselling and Psychotherapy* (Sage, 2000) and *Counselling: the BACP Counselling Reader, vol. 2* (with Milner, Sage, 2001).

He edits a number of book series including *Stress Counselling* (Continuum) and *Brief Therapies* (Sage). He is Honorary Vice President of the Institute of Health Promotion and Education, and Honorary Vice President of the International Stress Management Association (UK).

He has been awarded by the British Psychological Society, Division of Counselling Psychology, the Annual Counselling Psychology Award for 'Outstanding professional and scientific contribution to Counselling Psychology in Britain for 2000'. Recently the Institute of Health Promotion and Education awarded him a Fellowship for his 'Outstanding contribution to the theory and practice of health promotion and health education'.

His interests include jazz, astronomy, walking, writing and art.

The Contributors

Malcolm C. Cross is a Chartered Counselling Psychologist, UKCP Registered Psychotherapist. He is currently the Director of the Counselling Psychology Programme at City University London.

Berni Curwen is a cognitive-behavioural psychotherapist accredited by the British Association of Behavioural and Cognitive Psychotherapies and registered with the United Kingdom Council for Psychotherapy. She has a psychiatric nurse background and has worked in both the NHS and private practice. She contributed two chapters to *Client Assessment* (Sage, 1997) and co-authored *Brief Cognitive Behaviour Therapy* (Sage, 2000).

John Davy is a Chartered Counselling, Educational and Health Psychologist. John works part-time in an NHS Child and Adolescent Mental Health Service, and as a research supervisor for City University's counselling psychology courses. He has particular interests in systemic therapy and cultural psychology, chronic illness, clinical and research supervision, writing and psychotherapy, and the social politics of ethical training and practice. John has a doctorate on the uses of deconstruction in counselling psychology, and is completing advanced training in family and systemic psychotherapy with the Institute of Family Therapy.

David Glass is a counselling psychologist in training. He is originally from Scotland but has studied in a variety of places: he completed his Bachelors in the USA and settled in London to pursue his career as a counsellor. Having completed his MSc in Counselling Psychology at City University, he is currently studying at London Guildhall University where he is en route to being a Chartered Counselling Psychologist. He has worked in a variety of clinical settings, including a child and family therapy centre and primary care practice, and at present works as a counsellor in substance misuse.

Diane Hammersley is a Chartered Counselling Psychologist working in independent practice. A former Chair of the BPS Division of Counselling Psychology, she takes a particular interest in the needs of trainees and new practitioners looking for employment opportunities.

Charles Legg is a Senior Lecturer in Psychology at City University. He initially trained as an experimental psychologist, specialising in brain and behaviour, but requalified as a Counselling Psychologist, attaining chartered status in 1995. He is interested in the impact of biological factors, such as obesity and drug use, on problem formation and resolution in counselling, the role of theory in Counselling Psychology, systems theory and postmodern approaches to Psychology.

Gladeana McMahon is a BACP Fellow and Senior Registered Practitioner, a BABCP Accredited Cognitive-Behavioural Psychotherapist and is UKCP and UKRC Ind. registered Counsellor. She is a part-time Senior Lecturer on the Diploma and Masters programmes at the University of East London and has written, co-authored or edited 16 books. Gladeana is Associate Editor of *Counselling*, Managing Editor of *Stress News* and Associate Editor of the *BABCP Newsletter*.

Linda Papadopoulos is a Chartered Health and Counselling Psychologist and a Senior Lecturer in Psychology at London Guildhall University. She has published widely in the field of medical psychology and psychodermatology and gives specialist lectures on working with clients with disfigurement and skin disease. She is course director of the MSc in Counselling Psychology at London Guildhall University, where she is also heading up a large-scale study into the psychological effects of skin disease in collaboration with dermatologists from St. Thomas' Hospital. She has worked in numerous health psychology and primary care settings and runs workshops with medical students on the psychological implications of illness. Her recent book on psychodermatology is considered a seminal text in the field.

Justin Parker is a Chartered Counselling Psychologist and an Associate Fellow of the British Psychological Society. He is a lecturer in psychology at London Guildhall University. He also works as a Senior Counselling Psychologist in the NHS and consultant to various primary care groups. He is currently conducting research into the effects of couple counselling upon adjustment to disfigurement.

Christine Parrott is a Chartered Counselling Psychologist. With an undergraduate degree from Dartmouth College in the United States, Christine moved to Britain in 1992 and earned her Masters and Post-

Masters Degree in Counselling Psychology at City University. She also has a Diploma in Applied Hypnosis from University College London. Recently, Christine returned to live in New York where she writes and is producing a psychology-based programme for television. Her special interests include parenting, evolutionary psychology and moral behaviour.

David G. Purves is a Senior Lecturer in Counselling Psychology at London Guildhall University and is a BPS Chartered Counselling Psychologist. Originally trained as an Experimental Neuroscientist, he has recently completed retraining in Counselling Psychology and Psychotherapy. David combines lecturing with a private practice and working as a specialist in psychological trauma at a dedicated NHS clinic. His research interests centre around understanding the development of responses to trauma and treatment of PTSD.

Susanne Robbins has an MSc in Counselling Psychology at London Guildhall University and is currently studying for a Post MSc Diploma in Counselling Psychology, also at London Guildhall University. She obtained her first degree from the Open University and is also a Registered Nurse. She is particularly interested in counselling people coping with physical illness or disability.

Peter Ruddell is a cognitive-behavioural psychotherapist accredited by the British Association of Behavioural and Cognitive Psychotherapies and registered with the United Kingdom Council for Psychotherapy. He has worked in both the voluntary sector and private practice. He contributed two chapters to *Client Assessment* (Sage, 1997) and co-authored *Brief Cognitive Behaviour Therapy* (Sage, 2000).

Kasia Szymanska is a Chartered Counselling Psychologist, a BABCP Accredited Psychotherapist and is also UKCP registered. She works in private practice, for a Stress Unit in the City of London and as a lecturer in counselling psychology. She also works as a trainer and is the editor of *Counselling Psychology Review*, published by the British Psychological Division of Counselling Psychology. She is an Associate Director of the Centre for Stress Management, London.

Jill D. Wilkinson is a Chartered Counselling and Chartered Health Psychologist of the British Psychological Society. Over the last decade she has taken an active part in the development of Counselling Psychology in the UK. She is a former Senior Examiner and is the current Chair of the BPS Board of Examiners for the professional qualifying examination (the BPS Diploma in Counselling Psychology) for Chartered Status of the BPS. Until 1999 she was Senior Lecturer

and Course Director of the Practitioner Doctorate (PsychD) in Psychotherapeutic and Counselling Psychology at the University of Surrey,
where she continues to do some lecturing. For the past 20 years she
has also worked in independent therapeutic practice.

Ray Woolfe is a Chartered Counselling Psychologist, Psychoanalytic
Psychotherapist (registered with UKCP) and an accredited Counsellor
(registered with UKRC). He is a fellow of BACP and practises as a
Psychologist and Psychotherapist in Manchester. He has written
widely about counselling and psychology and after retiring from a
career as senior lecturer in counselling studies at Keele University, is
professor in counselling psychology at London Guildhall University.

Introduction

Robert Bor and Stephen Palmer

Every year, hundreds of people in the UK start their training to become counsellors, psychotherapists or counselling psychologists. In addition, many thousands in other countries and regions throughout the world, the USA, Canada, Australia, New Zealand, South Africa and the European Union, also start on this road. Counselling skills are also taught in fields allied to counselling and psychotherapy, such as medicine, nursing, law, physiotherapy, teaching and child guidance, to name but a few. Some professionals within these fields aspire to specialist counselling and psychotherapy training. If you are thinking about professional training in one of these fields, this book has been written with you in mind. Our aim is to help you make decisions about the path your studies will follow and to help you to prepare your application for the selection interview. This book is also designed for trainers, tutors, supervisors and other professionals who carry the responsibility of mentoring our future colleagues.

Counselling, psychotherapy and counselling psychology are rapidly becoming professions in their own right. In the new millennium, it is increasingly likely that the terms 'counsellor', 'psychotherapist' and 'psychologist' will be restricted for use by those who have undergone a recognised professional training programme in one of the professions. Furthermore, they will be obliged to adhere to a code of practice and ethics set out by an overseeing body, and agree to participate in lifelong professional development. Training requirements have become increasingly stringent due to the rapid increase in professionalism in the field of counselling.

There is growing competition for places on training courses. Demand for qualified and well-trained graduates is also reflected in the profiles of those who get offered jobs. The days where someone with a rudimentary training and relevant counselling experience can hope to secure a good job have long gone. Training to become a counsellor, psychotherapist or counselling psychologist is both rigorous and intense. In recent years we have witnessed fervent activity within these fields aimed at (a) defining their knowledge base and training requirement; (b) establishing licensing and accreditation bodies; (c) setting out the requirements for ongoing training, supervision and professional development; and (d) implementing and enforcing a code for professional conduct in practice.

One might argue that the demands placed on trainees are not altogether unreasonable. After all, as a modern counsellor you will require many qualities including stamina, will power, motivation, adaptability, empathy, humour and a quick wit. You will also need to keep up to date with research and developments in the field, supervise and train more junior colleagues and manage caseloads.

If you are aspiring to become a counsellor, psychotherapist or counselling psychologist, you will need to make decisions about your training and future career. Students have told us in several different contexts that it has often proved difficult to make decisions about their training with only limited information available. Applicants to courses typically have many different questions but no reliable source to answer some of the more important ones. Obviously, each course has its own entry qualifications and requirements and readers should ensure that at least they familiarise themselves with these.

There are some generic questions, which can help you to be better informed when it comes to selecting and applying to a training course. In this text, we have endeavoured to cover the issues and concerns that occupy many course applicants. Hopefully, you will find the contents interesting and the style relaxed. Each contributor is an experienced practitioner who has undergone a professional training at some stage of their career. All have some involvement with the selection and training of students.

In Chapter 1, Ray Woolfe briefly explains how a trainee can become fully qualified through one of the three key professional organisations: British Association for Counselling and Psychotherapy (BACP); United Kingdom Council for Psychotherapy (UKCP); the British Psychological Society (BPS). Then he covers how a training route can be selected. This chapter provides an excellent overview to the overlapping professions and their accrediting systems. It sets the scene for the rest of the book.

The next three chapters focus on the key professional bodies in more depth. Gladeana McMahon (Chapter 2) explains the new BACP accreditation procedure. She gives her personal view regarding the advantages of being accredited, which include receiving additional counselling referrals. The UKCP consists of eight sections and additional members. In Chapter 3, Kasia Szymanska and Stephen Palmer describe these different parts and also provide information about the different types of therapy offered by each section. They believe that there may be more competition from other professional organisations such as the BACP or the BPS and this could affect their status as the main umbrella for psychotherapy. Chapter 4, by Jill Wilkinson, examines and explores routes to becoming a Chartered Counselling Psychologist. She suggests that by reading professional counselling psychology journals, prospective trainees can discover what staff and trainees are publishing and thereby find out the research interests of those involved in the course. This may help in deciding which course to choose.

In Chapter 5, Linda Papadopoulos and Justin Parker describe the three main theoretical models of psychological counselling: psycho-analytic, humanistic and cognitive-behavioural therapies. Each section includes the history, theoretical concepts, therapeutic process, and the limitations, highlighting the commonalities and differences between the various approaches. In fact, a basic understanding of these is often important when being interviewed for training courses. In Chapter 6, Peter Ruddell and Berni Curwen discuss the personal qualities of a competent counsellor. They include issues such as time management skills, stamina, genuineness and flexibility. Therapist humour is also covered, noting that it can be an important catalyst in helping clients to see situations or problems from a more constructive perspective.

The next two chapters focus on preparing for the course application and the subsequent interview. In Chapter 7 Charles Legg highlights that any kind of selection, whether for a job or a course, can be a harrowing experience. The focus of the chapter is on those readers who want to communicate accurately in their applications, not those who wish to mislead. Although there is no magic formula for completing forms and being accepted onto a course, Legg has covered the main methods to help applicants represent themselves in a constructive light. In Chapter 8, Christine Parrott develops this theme further on the preparation for a training course interview. We are reminded of the old saying, 'You never have a second chance to make a first impression'. Therefore, appearance, body language and our knowledge about the particular course are important. In addition, the different types of interview are covered such as individual, group or panel interviews. In Chapter 9, Kasia Szymanska addresses trainee expectations of courses as compared to the reality of training experiences and seeks to offer a balanced view of what you might reasonably expect from becoming a trainee.

The next two chapters assume that you have managed to pass the earlier hurdles and are now attending a course. In Chapter 10, Malcolm Cross and David Glass focus on helpful study habits and include issues such as participating in lectures, small group discussions known as seminars, tutorials and maintaining reflective journals. Many students suffer from exam nerves which can be quite debilitating for some, leading to very high levels of stress. This particular problem and exam technique are addressed.

In recent years, there has been an increase in therapeutic training providers expecting trainees to enter therapy for the duration of the course. This has largely arisen due to the BACP, BPS and the majority of member organisations of the UKCP making personal therapy mandatory. In Chapter 11, John Davy outlines the arguments which have been made for and against this requirement, and offers guidance on arranging personal therapy. In addition, some cautionary guidance is given on how to avoid problems in therapy and the possible different expectations of both therapist and trainee.

Chapter 12 describes two trainees' perspectives of psychological counselling training. People considering entering this profession may find that reading this chapter provides a useful insight into what they may experience while attending a programme. Susie Robbins and David Purves share some of their fears and the challenges they encountered. For example, Robbins had not expected the course to be so demanding, whereas Purves sometimes felt that he knew more about psychology than some of his tutors in the first year of his course. Although this chapter has been positioned near the end of the book as the chapters have been arranged in a logical manner, it may still be worth dipping into at an early stage.

So, what does happen after you have finished your training and become fully qualified? When you go into practice, if you do not look after yourself, you could experience burnout. You may need to select a new supervisor or you may wish to enter private practice. In Chapter 13, Diane Hammersley covers a range of these issues including finding a job and continuing professional development. She brings this book to a conclusion by reminding us to 'Enjoy your career, the fulfilment it may bring you, and the privilege of knowing yourself and other in such a special way'.

The book concludes with a Recommended Reading list for trainees or prospective trainees and an Appendix of the main professional organisations mentioned in this book.

For ease and simplicity, the terms 'counsellor', 'therapist' and 'psychologist' are used interchangeably in this book. We do not wish to antagonise readers who may hold firm views about the apparent differences between these groups, but we believe that since they are all closely 'related' it is appropriate to avoid repeating all three wherever they appear. Clients and counsellors are also interchangeably referred to as 'he' and 'she'. These titles do not reflect any bias on the part of the authors but are merely convenient terms.

We wish you luck in your application and trust that the course you find is both stimulating and enjoyable. A related new text *The Trainee Handbook* (edited by Bor & Watts, 1999) may be a valuable resource for those starting their training and who require guidance in many of the practical aspects of their training such as finding a practice placement, planning their research, writing case studies and process reports, and finding a job, among many other topics.

REFERENCE

Bor, R. and Watts, M. (1999) The Trainee Handbook: a guide for counselling and psychotherapy trainees. London: Sage.

1

Training Routes into Therapy

Ray Woolfe

The question: How do I train to become a counsellor or counselling psychologist or psychotherapist? appears to be simple and straight-forward, but in reality is considerably more complex than it appears at first sight. Underlying this complexity is the fact that we are not talking about a single unified profession. To simplify the discussion I shall use the generic terms 'therapy' and 'therapists' to denote the entire domain.

The world of therapy is peopled by a large number of related but different professions. These include counsellors, psychotherapists, counselling psychologists, psychoanalysts, psychiatrists, mental health nurses, community psychiatric nurses, nurse therapists, clinical psychologists, hypnotherapists, art therapists, dramatherapists and psychodramatists. This list is by no means exhaustive.

It should also be noted that the term 'profession' is being used here fairly loosely. Traditionally the term refers to an occupation based upon a distinct body of knowledge, with clearly defined standards of entry and regulated by a body such as the General Medical Council or United Kingdom Council for Nursing, Midwifery and Health Visiting. In the UK, the most explicit recognition of a profession is when there is statutory regulation where a formal register exists, as in the case of the two examples cited above. The register is controlled by members of the profession which is self-regulating. Some professions, though not statutorily regulated, have established voluntary registers, for example, the Register of Chartered Psychologists held by the British Psychological Society while the United Kingdom Register of Counsellors (UKRC) offers a similar scheme for counsellors and the United Kingdom Council for Psychotherapy (UKCP) offers the same facility for psychotherapists. A bill to regulate psychological therapies was well advanced until the dissolution of Parliament for the 2001 election. This is likely to be resurrected in the new Parliament and statutory regulation may become a reality as early as 2003.

BOUNDARIES

The boundaries between these groups are by no means watertight. Many people would claim adherence to more than one group. From the perspective of the individual receiving assistance, the label of the person one sees and the sort of help given can be bewildering and is often heavily influenced by chance. Even the kind of label attached to the recipient of help, such as client or patient, can be arbitrary. It may depend upon such factors as the source of referral, the individual's workplace, whether there is an associated physical illness or condition, financial status, the existence of health insurance and age. It is not surprising, therefore, that the general public is confused and that this confusion is reflected among individuals seeking training and qualifications.

A recent survey on psychotherapy services within the National Health Service in England (NHS Executive, 1996) is indicative of the complexity. It states that 'one of the most striking findings of our investigation has been the degree of confusion surrounding the meaning of the term "psychotherapy". The survey reveals that the term is being used within the NHS to describe three different approaches to psychological intervention. One refers to psychological treatment as an integral component of mental health care. An example might be a community psychiatric nurse helping a patient to manage feelings of depression. A second that is described as 'eclectic psychological therapy and counselling' involves a treatment intervention which may be informed by more than one theoretical framework. An example might be a counsellor linked to a primary health care practice. The third approach, described as 'formal psychotherapies', is practised within specific models, with clearly defined protocols for practice. These interventions are often based in designated psychotherapy units and mostly employ either psychodynamic/analytical or cognitive behavioural methodologies.

The lack of clear boundaries can be confusing for potential entrants to the field of therapy. Were we to begin from scratch, with a clean slate in creating a new universe of therapy, it is likely that we would arrive at a more simplified structure than the one which we now possess. However, in the world in which we live there are few clear boundaries. We can identify that to become a psychiatrist a medical qualification is required; to become a counselling or clinical psychologist an initial psychological qualification is necessary and community psychiatric nurses have to be nurses. But these are exceptions rather than the rule and the labels 'counsellor' and 'psychotherapist' are fraught with complexity. The confusion extends to potential employers as well as trainees.

COUNSELLING AND PSYCHOTHERAPY

The confusion over boundaries is nowhere more apparent than in addressing the task of differentiating between the activity known as psychotherapy and that known as counselling. While some argue that the two are completely different, others insist that there are no essential differences and use the two terms interchangeably. Elsewhere, in exploring the future prospects for counselling (Woolfe, 1997), I have suggested that attempts to distinguish between the two terms usually contain some or all of the points which follow below. I have provided this list, not because I necessarily agree with all its components, but so that you may make more informed choices if you are seeking training to become a counsellor or psychotherapist. The arguments run as follows:

- Psychotherapy is concerned with personality change, whereas counselling is concerned with helping individuals to utilise their own coping resources. The former can be seen as reconstructive and the latter as facilitative.

- Psychotherapists work with people who manifest significant emotional disturbances. Counsellors, however, work with people who are basically emotionally healthy but who are experiencing temporary problems. These are associated with events such as stress at work, relationship breakdown or bereavement. They also involve life-cycle, developmental phenomena such as coping with the experience of children leaving home or feeling odd if one remains single at the age of 30 when all one's friends are married.

- Whereas most counsellors work with clients in a consciously experienced here-and-now relationship, many psychotherapists would acknowledge the phenomenon of transference and actively work with it. This acknowledges that a relationship between the two parties contains many unconscious elements. However, psychotherapy incorporates practitioners operating from a variety of theoretical orientations and many, such as cognitive-behavioural workers, would dispute this proposition.

- Psychotherapy tends to be long term, while counselling is of shorter term duration.

- Personal analysis is at the heart of much psychotherapy training, (though not cognitive-behavioural) whereas counselling training places more emphasis upon the acquisition of specific skills.

- Arguably, the dominant orientations among psychotherapists are psychodynamic and cognitive-behavioural, whereas the dominant orientation among counsellors is person centred. There are detailed accounts of these various approaches in another chapter of this book.

- The organisations which employ psychotherapists are primarily clinical and medical and often located within the NHS. In contrast, counsellors are more frequently to be found in educational institutions and the workplace or in the voluntary sector. It follows from this that psychotherapists tend to work with patients and counsellors with clients. Once again, however, there is no hard and fast rule. For example, many counsellors are now employed, though mostly on a part-time basis, within the primary health care sector of the NHS.

TRAINING ROUTES

In practice, whereas training routes into counselling are open to anybody who can demonstrate a reasonable quality of self-awareness and is prepared to persevere, training routes into psychotherapy careers are more complex. They frequently involve building upon an existing qualification in fields such as nursing, occupational therapy, psychiatry and psychology. Even with these professional qualifications, some form of preparatory training in counselling or counselling skills is often required before individuals are accepted into psychotherapy training. The fact that some pre-existing qualification may be needed means that a qualification in psychotherapy may represent a form of added value to many individuals and (like counselling) does not necessarily offer a whole career in itself.

This is particularly the case with people employed in the NHS. The survey carried out by the NHS Executive (1996: 71) states that 'the multi-disciplinary nature of all types of psychotherapy provision creates a complex situation for training'. Such persons may be able to engage in psychotherapy training and achieve UKCP registration without any counselling training. However, for lay persons without this medical or medical linked background, it would be more difficult to get a place on a respectable psychotherapy training programme without first gaining a counselling qualification.

COUNSELLING AS A CAREER

Counselling is a diffuse activity and programmes of training in counselling reflect this diversity. The key organisation in the field is the British Association for Counselling and Psychotherapy (BACP), which all trainee counsellors would be well advised to join. It offers a code of ethics as well as providing a sense of belonging to a wider community. The use of the word 'counselling' and not 'counsellors' is significant and represents the organisation's acknowledgement that counselling is a broad church, comprising more than those people practising professionally as counsellors. It also reflects a commitment to represent the interests of the whole of what is a very heterogeneous constituency. The constituency might be seen to contain three main cohorts.

First, there are those people who may be employed specifically as counsellors and whom we might describe as professional counsellors. Student counselling is traditionally the most professionalised sector within counselling and indeed the Association for Student Counselling (one of the divisions of BACP) existed prior to the birth of the latter and originally offered its own accreditation scheme. However, the number of people employed on a full-time basis specifically as a counsellor is very limited. Jobs offered in fields such as substance abuse may demand an additional professional qualification such as nursing. An increasing number of jobs are coming on tap within the primary health care sector, although these are frequently on a part-time basis. Any individual seeking a career in counselling should be fully aware of the magnitude of the task. A concept such as the profession of counselling offering a career with a clear and recognised pay structure and prospects of promotion does not exist in the same way as we might think of nursing, social work or teaching as professions which offer careers.

Second, and somewhat larger than the cohort of professional counsellors, is a vast army of people who use counselling skills in the course of their paid work as social workers, nurses, teachers, youth workers, community workers, doctors, psychologists, etc., though they are not designated as counsellors or employed specifically as such. There are a large number of courses focusing on counselling skills which cater for this market. They exist in universities, the further education sector and in private training institutes.

Third, there is another army of people who use counselling in the course of their work with voluntary agencies such as Mind, Relate, Victim Support, Rape Crisis, Cruse, etc. Sometimes a voluntary agency will offer its own training programme. These may be designed for beginning counsellors or they may be targetted at counsellors who have already received some training but wish to develop their expertise in a particular field such as bereavement and loss.

FINDING A TRAINING PROGRAMME

Individuals seeking to enter the profession, particularly if they have no other professional qualifications, are frequently faced with a dilemma commonly described as Catch 22 which generates great frustration. This can be expressed in the following form. To gain entry onto a course of training, it is often necessary to be able to demonstrate that one has some practical experience of counselling. However, at the same time, individuals seeking to gain that experience are frequently met with the response that they must first gain some qualification before they can be exposed to clients.

As I have already emphasised, in the case of counselling the term 'profession' is a misnomer if we define a profession as containing a recognised career path, a selection of jobs and agreed salary scales. However, for those who wish to persevere, the way forward is often to gain experience in a voluntary capacity. Some voluntary organisations will offer their own programmes of training which can then help the individual to gain acceptance onto higher level courses in educational institutions or private training institutes. A variety of such institutes exists, often focused around a particular theoretical orientation such as gestalt, transactional analysis, person centred, or psychodynamic. Persons seeking a guide to training courses are advised to consult *Training in Counselling and Psychotherapy*, published annually by BACP.

So far as these educational institutes and private training institutions are concerned, there is no uniformity or description of qualifications. There exists a wide variety of titles from certificates in counselling skills, to certificates in counselling, to diplomas, masters degrees and more recently to doctorates. In an ideal world, one would lead on to another in a laddering, hierarchical process. In practice, however, the situation is extraordinarily anarchic with some high level courses designated as certificates, some diploma courses offering intensive practical experience, while other diploma or masters courses are highly theoretical and would not claim to provide students with more than basic practitioner competence. There is no simple way for the novitiate to unravel these complexities. My advice is to shop around, talk to past or present students/trainees and study syllabuses and curricula carefully with particular attention to course aims and objectives, intended behavioural objectives and access offered on completion to UKRC, UKCP or other registration schemes.

THEORETICAL ORIENTATION

In selecting a course of training, the question of theoretical orientation should be borne in mind. To some extent, particularly outside the large metropolitan centres, this may be a matter of opportunity. If, for example, you live in a small town where the only training institution offers a person-centred training, your options may be limited. However, personality factors may also be important. For example, if you are a person who possesses a generally optimistic view of life, seeing it as full of exciting potential, you may be drawn towards a person-centred training rather than any other. Similarly if you perceive life in rather more tragic terms as involving coming to terms with childhood experiences you may find psychodynamic approaches particularly pertinent.

However, in addition to opportunity and personality other factors may influence decisions about theoretical orientation. Feltham (1997: 8) itemises no fewer than 15 reasons for theoretical allegiances. These include truth appeal, novelty, conservatism, selecting the best, eclecticism and certitude. In larger centres such as Manchester or London, there exists a vast variety of choice and potential trainees would do well to research the market.

This discussion is not academic. Different theoretical approaches emphasise different requirements and styles of teaching, in order to be congruent with the approach. Thus the theoretical orientation of the selected course may have a significant impact upon the kind of learning experience to which one is exposed. As Dryden and Thorne (1991) put it: 'the choice of training methods depends crucially upon the goals of that training . . . (and these goals) . . . will be inextricably linked with the trainers' view of the effective practitioner' (pp. 15–16).

Dryden and Thorne suggest that initial counselling training courses should provide trainees with learning opportunities in four main areas: self-exploration, supervised work with clients, the acquisition of counselling skills, and counselling theory and relevant academic material. In some programmes, the last of these categories could be extended to include the ability to understand research findings and to carry out basic research. The balance between all these aspects will vary across training programmes.

On a person-centred training programme the emphasis is likely to be upon producing counsellors who can manifest the core conditions of empathy, acceptance and congruence. On such a course, the key feature of person-centred practice – that the client knows what is best for her or him – is likely to be paralleled by an emphasis on student-centred learning. This asserts that the individual student knows best what his or her learning needs are. Tutor and student will be involved in a relationship in which mutuality and equality is emphasised. There is likely to be a significant amount of experiential work in groups allowing an opportunity to explore aspects of self and to experience the core conditions.

In contrast, a psychodynamic training is likely to emphasise extensive personal therapy/analysis for the trainee. This will be accompanied by a small number of long-term, heavily supervised cases. All trainees, whatever their theoretical orientation, should be aware that being a trainee can be an infantilising experience. However, this is especially the case with this particular orientation, where the process emphasises the re-awakening of childhood experiences through transference in the relationship between therapist and client. In this context, tutors are likely to become more parental/authority figures than would be experienced in the person-centred mode.

Training in a third format, the cognitive-behavioural mode, is likely to take yet another form. Here the concentration is likely to be on the development of executive skills such as functional analysis, brief therapeutic work and assessment. There is likely to be less emphasis on personal development, whether through personal developmental groups as in the person-centred mode or personal therapy as in the psychodynamic mode. In the cognitive-behavioural mode of therapy, the therapist is likely to adopt a fairly didactic teaching role in relation to the client and this is likely to be paralleled in the relationship between tutor and student.

These are just snapshot pictures and many counselling courses would now claim to be adopting a more integrative approach across orientations. However, it is not always clear what this term means in practice. Integrative is a modern buzzword (and and) prospective trainees would do well to explore the meaning of this concept if it is presented as a significant aspect of a training programme.

COUNSELLING ACCREDITATION

The moral of the story I have so far described is that undergoing training in order to achieve qualifications in counselling and becoming accredited is not an automatic pathway to a job and a career. However, the purpose of training is to achieve a standard and the gold standard for those persons who would seek to find work as counsellors is accreditation to become what is now called a 'Registered Practitioner'.

The accreditation scheme is offered by BACP and accreditation is the basis for eligibility for inclusion in a UK Register of Counsellors to become what is now called a 'Registered Practitioner'. The register began to list individual counsellors in 1996 and now operates at two levels. An individual can register provided that they are accredited by either BACP or the Confederation of Scottish Counselling Agencies (COSCA). There is also, however, since 1998, provision for organisations to register provided that they satisfy the basic criteria. Ideally, all counsellors working within such organisations would be eligible for accreditation as individuals, but in practice this is unlikely.

While I have emphasised the importance of accreditation for those who would seek a career in counselling, progress towards it can be complex. At the present time, there exist three routes towards accreditation. They apply to counsellors working with individuals or couples and not to group counselling. In considering the concept of accreditation, it is helpful to envisage it as comprising two components: training and practice.

The first route involves completion of a course accredited by BACP plus 450 hours of counselling practice supervised on the basis of not less than one and a half hours per month. An accredited course (formerly called a recognised course) satisfies the training component of accreditation. However, while some clinical practice will be accumulated during the course, it is unlikely that sufficient hours will have been accumulated to satisfy the practice component. It is probable, therefore, that some or even the bulk of the necessary experience is likely to be obtained after the completion of the course.

A variant of this route involves undertaking 450 hours of counselling training comprising skills development (200 hours) and theory (250 hours) plus at least 450 hours of practice over a minimum period of three years. The essential difference between the two methods is that an applicant for accreditation who has completed an accredited course does not have to demonstrate that they have satisfied the training criteria. In all other cases, this will be necessary.

A second route is designed for persons who may claim little course-based training, but who can provide evidence of ten years experience of counselling with a minimum of 150 practice hours per year under formal supervision. In addition, the most recent three years must include 450 hours of practice supervised on the basis of at least one and a half hours per month.

A third route occupies a middle position and asks for a combination of some formal training and practice.

In addition to all the above criteria, there is a requirement for continuing formal supervision of at least one and a half hours per month; of serious commitment to ongoing personal and professional development; and of at least 40 hours of personal counselling.

An examination of advertisements for such full-time jobs as exist in counselling (see *The Guardian* each Tuesday and Wednesday) will reveal that applicants are being asked to provide BACP accreditation or to demonstrate that they are working towards accreditation. In this climate, there is an incentive for courses to seek accreditation. As more courses do so, the process of defining professional standards gathers pace and the likelihood of statutory regulation for psychological therapies in a few years will accelerate the process.

NATIONAL VOCATIONAL QUALIFICATIONS (NVQS)

It would not be appropriate to discuss training routes in counselling without saying something about National Vocational Qualifications

(NVQs). In 1986 the government established the National Council for Vocational Qualifications in order to improve the number and level of qualifications among the workforce. The aim of this body was to oversee the development of qualifications linked to occupational standards. In 1994, it set up an Advice, Guidance, Counselling and Psychotherapy Lead Body to set standards and qualifications for all those involved in these fields. The new qualifications are to be expressed in terms of the competencies required for working in these fields at various levels.

The effect of NVQs is to emphasise output in the form of competence in action rather than input in the form of academic qualification as the basis for certification. BACP is likely to acknowledge NVQs as an additional way of satisfying accreditation requirements. It is possible that counselling training programmes will become increasingly focused on the delivery of an NVQ. Funding incentives are likely to facilitate this process as governments increasingly perceive educational programmes not as ends in themselves but as steps towards competence in the workplace.

UNITED KINGDOM COUNCIL FOR PSYCHOTHERAPY (UKCP)

The nature of counselling training can vary greatly according to the theoretical orientation of a course. The question of orientation assumes even greater significance in the field of psychotherapy training. The field contains three major traditions: psychoanalytical/psychodynamic, cognitive-behavioural and humanistic/existential. While there is a growing interest in integration, the fact remains that training institutes (as they tend to describe themselves) tend to adhere to one or other approach.

The role of the UK Register of Counsellors in the world of counselling is paralleled in psychotherapy by the United Kingdom Council for Psychotherapy (UKCP) inaugurated in 1993. The UKCP controls a national register and while this is voluntary it is seen as a step on the road to statutory registration. Only therapists who meet the training requirements of UKCP are included on the register.

Membership of the UKCP is organisational, not individual. There are approximately 80 members grouped together in autonomous sections representing all the main traditions in the practice of psychotherapy. At the present time there are eight sections. These are:

• Psychoanalytic and Psychodynamic Psychotherapy
• Behavioural and Cognitive Psychotherapy
• Family, Couple, Sexual and Systemic Therapy

- Humanistic and Integrative Psychotherapy
- Hypno-Psychotherapy
- Analytical Psychology
- Psychoanalytically-based Therapy with Children
- Experiential Constructivist Therapies.

Each section acts as the arbiter for their own branch of psychotherapy.

The implication of this structure is that to train as a psychotherapist so that one becomes registered by the UKCP it is necessary to satisfy the standards laid down by one of the member organisations. If an individual's professional background falls within any of these categories, it may be that an organisation exists that can accredit them for registration. However, for those seeking training, this may involve becoming a trainee within the particular organisation or one of its constituent agencies.

Training is usually for a minimum of three years and most involve a period of personal therapy. In some cases, particularly in the psychoanalytical field, the requirement for this can be quite extensive.

While systems exist for attempting to ensure comparability across sections, almost inevitably differences do exist in relation to entry requirements. These may concern necessary prior training in counselling or psychotherapy, membership of a particular profession such as medicine, nursing or psychology, or whether one works in a setting such as the NHS. The annual BACP handbook, *Training in Counselling and Psychotherapy*, offers the best general guide to the training that is available.

Trainees thinking about employment in a psychotherapy capacity within the NHS should also be aware that membership of some sections carries greater weight than others in terms of employment potential. As a general rule, psychodymic/analytical and cognitive-behavioural trainings are likely to be most favoured.

COUNSELLING PSYCHOLOGY

Professions are not static and in recent years a major newcomer has entered the field of counselling training: counselling psychology. Counselling has always been subject to the accusation that it is based upon faith rather than evidence, that it is an art rather than a science. It is difficult to demonstrate that it actually attains the outcomes which it claims to achieve. At the same time, psychology has been criticised for being over-scientific and that in trying to ape medicine it has lost sight of the therapeutic relationship at the heart of helping. The development of counselling psychology can be seen as deriving from a desire to integrate these two positions. It represents an acknowledgement that it is possible to place the working alliance between therapist and client at the heart of therapy, yet at the same time accepting the need to evaluate one's work and to base one's practice upon sound evidence.

The British Psychological Society (BPS) holds a register of chartered psychologists. To become a chartered psychologist one needs to have an initial qualification in psychology which confers what is known as the 'graduate basis for registration'. When followed by three years professional training and practice, chartered status is achieved. If this training and practice is in a specific field such as clinical or educational psychology, it is possible for the individual to use that adjectival title, hence, for example, chartered clinical psychologist. In 1992 the Society agreed that psychologists who had undergone therapeutic training should be given recognition for that training and suitably qualified persons were allowed to describe themselves as chartered counselling psychologists.

There are two routes to achieving this status. The first is as an independent trainee; the second is by doing an accredited course. For the former, a Diploma in Counselling Psychology offered by the BPS is the goal.

BPS DIPLOMA IN COUNSELLING PSYCHOLOGY

There are two steps. First, one must qualify for the Society's 'graduate basis for registration' (GBR). This involves receiving a satisfactory first degree in psychology or passing the Society's qualifying examination. Once this has been done, the individual is eligible to apply for enrolment as a candidate for the Society's Diploma in Counselling Psychology. This is in effect a Professional Qualifying Examination in Counselling Psychology.

The diploma is not a course. What it offers is a set of criteria concerning training and practice which must be satisfied if an individual is to receive chartered status as a counselling psychologist. As such it can be described as a yardstick against which an individual can measure her or his progress towards satisfying the diploma requirements. Put another way, it can be thought of as a template onto which the person can map their training and qualifications.

The diploma involves three years full-time study and practice or its part-time equivalent. It is possible to apply for prior accreditation for one or more of the components of the diploma, which would mean that completion might take less than three years. Prior accreditation is only possible for work completed after the receipt of GBR. The BPS argues that the application of psychological theory and insight to the practice of counselling can only happen in a systematic and conscious manner after the receipt of GBR.

Each student enrolled for the diploma is expected to find a co-ordinator of training who acts as a mentor, guide and advocate as the individual gradually works through both the academic and practical criteria which comprise the diploma.

ACCREDITED COURSES

The alternative to the independent route is by doing an accredited course. A number of courses have been accredited as satisfying the requirements of the diploma or just Part 1 (the diploma contains two parts). Students who succesfully complete a course accredited for both parts thus automatically become chartered as counselling psychologists.

However, the number of such courses, particularly outside the London region, is still limited and many trainees thus choose to proceed along an independent route. Where a course is only accredited against Part 1, students who take such a course can then take Part 2 via the independent route.

Many psychology departments within the NHS now look to counselling psychologists as potential employees. Moreover, discussions formally to recognise the profession of counselling psychology within the NHS are at an advanced state. This process has been facilitated by a general shortage of clinical psychologists. In some situations, counselling psychologists compete with counsellors for work, particularly in Primary Care trusts and groups.

SELECTING A TRAINING ROUTE

It was pointed out earlier, in respect of the different theoretical orientations, that training consists of a mixture of:

(a) self-exploration in the form of personal therapy, personal development groups, etc.
(b) supervised work with clients
(c) the acquisition of specific skills
(d) understanding theory and perhaps also making sense of and carrying out research.

It was also stated that the balance of these items may well differ across orientations. It is helpful for prospective trainees to bear this information in mind more generally in making choices.

Courses which offer similar qualifications will place different emphases on theory and practice. Counselling, it should be remembered, is both an education and a training. Courses in the university sector, perhaps inevitably, may tend to place greater emphasis on the former than do courses based in private training institutes or in therapeutic settings in the public sector such as NHS clinics. The balance between education and training in psychotherapy is arguably more generally loaded towards the latter. However, it is not easy to make exact statements. As always, what is important in making choices is to ensure that one has access to all the available information.

GETTING SELECTED

Some practicalities

Some tips which may be useful (see also other chapters of this book) are as follows:

1   Be clear about why you are applying to do training in counselling/psychotherapy/counselling psychology. The classic 'wanting to help people' is not likely to persuade in a positive direction.
2   Be clear about why you want to do the particular type of training (e.g. theoretical orientation) for which you are applying.
3   Be clear about why you want to do the particular course for which you are applying in the particular institution to which you are applying. Course directors like to know that their course has not been selected at random.
4   While it is normal for applicants to want to work out personal issues through counselling training, the trainer will be looking for evidence that work on such issues has already begun elsewhere and is ongoing.
5   Demonstrate that you have thought about the time implications of doing the particular course. The trainer will be looking for evidence that you have thought this through and have discussed it with partners and managers at work. Do you have the support of your managers?
6   Demonstrate that you are aware of the costs of training and are able to meet these costs.
7   Be able to show a degree of self-awareness in relation to one's strengths and limitations as a counsellor and as a learner.

CONCLUSION

For those individuals who wish to train as therapists without some other recognised professional qualification, the road can be long, costly and with no firm guarantee of employment at the end of it. Training involves not just the cost of tuition fees, but additional requirements for supervision, personal therapy, books and journals, professional indemnity insurance and membership of professional bodies such as BACP and BPS.

Persons who want to train as counsellors because they see therapy as a career are best discouraged. Feltham (1993) discusses making a living as a counsellor and comments that 'I, and most other counsellors I know, cannot rely on income purely from counselling private clients'. So while trainees must have a high degree of self-awareness and a commitment to personal development, perhaps the most important qualities of all reside in that complex of dispositions known as motivation, commitment and perseverence.

REFERENCES

British Association for Counselling and Psychotherapy (BACP) (2000). *Training in counselling and psychotherapy: a directory*. Rugby: BACP.

Dryden, W., & Thorne, B. (1991). *Training and supervision for counselling in action*. London: Sage.

Feltham, C. (1993). Making a living as a counsellor. In W. Dryden (Ed.), *Questions and answers on counselling in action*. London: Sage.

Feltham, C. (1997). Introduction: irreconcilable psychotherapies. In C. Feltham (Ed.), *Which psychotherapy?* London: Sage.

National Health Service Executive (1996). *NHS psychotherapy services in England: review of strategic policy*. London: NHS Executive.

Woolfe, R. (1997). Counselling in Britain: present position and future prospects. In S. Palmer & G. McMahon (Eds), *Handbook of counselling*. London: Routledge.

2

British Association for Counselling and Psychotherapy (BACP) Accreditation

Gladeana McMahon

BACP BACKGROUND

As the use of counsellors, paid or unpaid, began to increase during the late 1970s and early 1980s, many organisations and individuals became confused at the range of counselling qualifications and models of counselling training available in the UK. The general public also faced the same dilemma when locating a counsellor in private practice. These difficulties centred around the lack of any national mechanism to identify baseline skill and experience levels which organisations and individuals could look to as evidence of ability when selecting counsellors.

In 2000, the British Association for Counselling changed its name to the British Association for Counselling and Psychotherapy (BACP). For simplicity, in this chapter, when referring to the organisation, the new name will be used throughout.

In 1983, the British Association for Counselling and Psychotherapy (BACP) introduced what has probably become one of the best known schemes for the assessment and recognition of professional competence (Frankland, 1997). Following the success of the individual counsellor accreditation scheme, BACP introduced similar schemes for the accreditation of counselling supervisors (1988), counselling courses (1988) and counselling trainers (1997). However, not everyone has welcomed the introduction of accreditation. A body of opinion exists that believes accreditation has more to do with the medicalisation of counselling, rigid bureaucracy and elitism than with establishing professional standards related to client safety (Gibbon, 1990;

Mowbray, 1995). Alternative organisations such as the Independent Practitioner's Network (IPN) have come into being espousing what they believe to be a new model of accountability based on peer pressure and group responsibility in ensuring good practice (Totton, 1997).

Accreditation is not a statutory requirement to practise as a counsellor, nor is it seen in many circles as a measure of superiority over non-accredited and experienced counsellors. However, being accredited, working towards accreditation or having an equivalent form of recognition such as BPS or UKCP registration is now a usual requirement sought by employers and therefore carries status (Schapira, 2000). Nonetheless, BACP would also be among the first to assert that while accreditation minimises the likelihood of poor practice it cannot, as is the case with any other form of recognition, be seen as a 100 per cent guarantee of good practice (Wilkins & Frankland, 1997).

Some counsellors approach the process of accreditation with excitement, enjoying the opportunity it offers to reflect on personal practice, consider methods used to evaluate and assess practice and feel more involved with the accrediting organisation. A number of counsellors believe that accreditation reflects the sense that a senior practitioner stage of development has been achieved. Other counsellors see the process of accreditation as complex and complicated (Wilkins & Frankland, 1997).

There are currently three routes to counsellor accreditation and accreditation with the BACP is currently only available for work with individuals or couples and does not apply to group or family counselling. This situation is likely to change as accreditation for a range of counselling specialisms and counselling contexts moves towards validating those who work in them – for example, trauma and substance misuse counselling and/or counselling at work or in medical settings.

The accreditation process has been continually modified since its inception. Originally, there were only two routes by which a counsellor could become accredited. The first was through formal training of not less than 450 hours and the second was through the experienced practitioner route. Many counsellors were trained at a time when no formal certification of such courses took place and many counsellors had been practising successfully for a number of years. The experienced practitioner route, sometimes called the 'Ten Year Clause' (Frankland, 1995), was aimed at this group of people and required a minimum of ten years continued counselling practice to qualify. This scheme will be formally withdrawn at the end of 2001. Counselling supervision in line with the BACP Code of Ethics and Practice of 1.5 hours per month, minimum annual client contact hours of 150 per year, the provision of two cases studies (only one study being required for those having successfully completed a BACP accredited counsellor training course), a personal philosophy of counselling, a diary of a recent month's work and a supervisor's and proposer's statement were among the range of additional factors required for both groups. In 1997 an additional 40 hours of personal therapy was introduced as a requirement for accreditation.

Over time it became clear that a significant group of counsellors was being unfairly penalised and unable to apply for accreditation even though they were more than competent to do so. These were people whose original training had been less than 450 hours and who had not been practising for ten years: for example, a counsellor who had 350 hours of training and had been practicising for six years. Even though this counsellor may have undertaken additional training under the auspices of continued professional development (CPD) which may have accounted for a further 300 hours, none of this could be taken into account under the scheme. As a result in 1994 BACP introduced what became known as the 'Middle Route'. This route introduced the concept of training and practice units and required the applicant to have a total of ten units, three of which had to be practice units to qualify.

Up until the end of 1999, each candidate's application for accreditation was forwarded for peer assessment to a team comprising three assessors and one convenor. Wherever possible, teams were balanced in terms of therapeutic orientations, experience and work setting. Applications were assessed four times a year usually in batches of six per assessment team. The assessors forwarded comments and queries to the convenor who, in turn, would action these as appropriate, collating the team's view of each candidate and whether the candidate's application had succeeded. A majority decision of three out of the four on the assessment team would be required for a successful application to go forward. Those candidates whose applications were not successful would receive a letter outlining the grounds on which the application was being rejected. Applicants had the right of appeal and approximately 50 per cent of applications were successful (Wilkins & Frankland, 1997).

If a counsellor is unsuccessful in his or her accreditation application, the candidate must either resubmit the entire application or, if only part of the application is identified as being below an acceptable standard, the counsellor can rework the section in question for resubmission. Some counsellors choose to invoke the appeals procedure. However, it is very rarely that the decision of the appeals panel has varied from that of the original assessors.

Accreditation lasts for five years and at the end of this period of time the counsellor then applies for re-accreditation. The counsellor is required to demonstrate the range of continued professional development (CPD) undertaken since the last application, together with the provision of details regarding client hours and counselling supervision received. In addition, a case study combining both the style of client work together with the way in which counselling supervision is used is also required.

THE PROS AND CONS OF ACCREDITATION – A PERSONAL VIEW

Two main issues are involved here: first, whether any form of accreditation process is worthwhile; second, whether the particular process or procedures adopted by BACP have validity. These are not easy questions to answer.

If one looks at other more long-established professions – medicine, law, engineering, teaching, scientific research, etc. – it is clear that both the acquisition of knowledge and the ability and motivation to apply such knowledge are important. How could a physician work without understanding bodily functions or a civil engineer operate without knowledge of the properties of the materials being used?

In all professions there is also a period or periods for practising, invariably under experienced supervision, before the individual is judged to be capable. The difficulty with counselling is that there is no universal or commonly accepted agreement as to exactly what the required body of knowledge is, nor is there common agreement as to techniques and approaches. As to personal characteristics and motivation, on which many counselling relationships thrive or founder, these are even more difficult to validate. Yet we can all remember from our schooldays the impact that a good teacher can have on our own development or the difference between a dedicated caring nurse and one who is merely going through the motions when we are in hospital.

With a new profession such as counselling, the body of knowledge has yet to stabilise sufficiently for people to be able to say 'yes, this is what has to be learnt and this is how to put it into practice'. Perhaps in ten, twenty or even fifty years' time there may be a far greater consensus than there is at present. However, in the meantime, this is no excuse to do nothing. The public image of counselling is important to all counsellors and, as their most representative body, BACP is obliged to attempt to set professional standards or define qualifying processes. It does not pretend to have found a definitive answer and, perhaps, never will. Medical training lasts for many, many years but doctors may still make mistakes.

The BACP accreditation procedures should therefore be viewed as part of a learning process which will be modified in the light of greater wisdom with the passing of time. Those who are opposed to such accreditation should continue to voice their opinions, hopefully constructively, so that processes can be adjusted to accommodate good practitioners.

My own experience is derived from learning on the job rather than from classroom teaching and I imagine this may well be the case for people in other professions. Nonetheless, theory provides an essential framework against which practice can be measured and in its turn be modified and improved as a result of practical experience.

As a counsellor who has been accredited with BACP since 1990, there is no doubt in my mind that being accredited has increased the number of clients referring themselves to me. As someone who has been operating a private practice full time since 1988, I have noticed that the last five years have shown an increase in clients seeking my services either solely or partly because of my accredited status. Perhaps it is no surprise that this should coincide with the drive that BACP has instigated together with other professional bodies in promoting a variety of forms of accreditation as mechanisms for minimising poor practice. Indeed, the media have picked up on the difference between an accredited and non-accredited counsellor and, in turn, have spread the message through newspaper articles and the support materials made available following television and radio programmes of a psychological nature.

I value my accreditation for two reasons. On a personal level, as having been accredited on three separate occasions (my original application and then re-accredited twice since then), it has always felt rewarding to know that the client work I do has been externally validated. On a business level, accreditation has been instrumental in assisting me to build and promote my private practice and in securing part-time teaching work in the counselling world. After having talked to a number of colleagues, my experiences appear to be consistent with a number of others.

I am also conscious of the responsibility accreditation places on me to ensure my work continues to be of the highest standard possible. I would not like to lose my accreditation; it is something I value personally that has opened up career opportunities which may have been harder to get if I had not been accredited.

ALTERNATIVES TO BACP ACCREDITATION

BACP accreditation represents one form of sanction for counsellors to practise in the UK. However, non-possession does not prevent other professionally qualified practitioners, psychiatrists, psychologists, etc., from using counselling techniques, nor indeed does it prevent any person from practising as a counsellor. Is this a good thing or not? Across the world there is great diversity in religious beliefs and practices, in legal systems, in medicine and in culturally and socially accepted norms of behaviour. Does the rightness or wrongness of such diversity constitute a meaningful question? Hopefully, we no longer regard such diversity as forms of heresy to be severely punished.

Even within a single country there is much diversity, particularly in subjects or professions which are not strictly science based. Different schools of thought exist and sometimes one school of thought is in the ascendant, sometimes another. Economics and sociology are two such examples. The 'correct' parenting of children is another. We live in an age of uncertainty where beliefs can and are questioned – not like 'the good old days' where everyone knew their place and what to believe and what was expected of them.

Notwithstanding all of this, there is still the matter of public acceptability, though it should be appreciated that 'the public' does not operate with a single view or opinion any more than those much abused beings 'society' or 'community'. It is probably fair to say that, at any point of time, there is a majority view or a broad consensus. Again, this may be an ignorant or ill-informed view but it is unwise to ignore its existence. There is little doubt in my mind that the average person does regard qualifications and accreditations as indicative, but not necessarily a guarantee of a basic competence in the first instance.

Thus, even with all the many reservations expressed above, the typical potential client or employer is likely to look favourably upon counsellors who can show that they have experienced a process of learning and achieved recognition by a recognised formal body set up for this purpose. At present, BACP is generally recognised as such a body.

It is quite possible that other organisations such as the Independent Practitioner Network (IPN) may achieve recognition as being a body competent in ensuring good practice among its members. Peer pressure and group accountability are powerful forces as any member of a sports team or close-knit family will testify. But, for good or ill, such pressures work only if its members work closely together as a group and have the time to influence each other. Geographical separation could be a major obstacle to cohesion and consistency.

Perhaps for those of us who are counsellors, undergoing super-vision and, possibly, personal therapy, we can use our own experi-ences to provide evidence as to how we choose our own supervisors or counsellors and whether we are satisfied with our choices. What value do we put on the possession of BACP accreditation by those whose services we use? Does our view depend on whether we our-selves are BACP accredited?

OTHER FORMS OF RECOGNITION

It is worth noting that the British Psychological Society (BPS) has a similar process of accreditation for members which is called charter-ship and that a body such as the British Association for Behavioural and Cognitive Psychotherapies has an accreditation process for cognitive-behavioural practitioners. Other bodies such as the United Kingdom Council for Psychotherapy (UKCP) and the United Kingdom Register of Counsellors (UKRC) were set up to provide another type of validation of counsellors and psychotherapists in an attempt to offer a baseline sense of validation of registered individuals. Many practitioners have chosen to become accredited with more than one body and it is not uncommon to find that someone who is accredited with BACP may also be chartered with BPS (if they are also a psychologist) or registered with either UKCP or UKRC.

THE NEW ACCREDITATION PROCEDURE

At the end of 1999, the peer assessment of accreditation ceased and the task of accreditation became the responsibility of a team of seven part-time paid assessors from a variety of therapeutic orientations. Many BACP members found themselves mourning the loss of the peer assessment process. However, an equal number welcomed what they saw as a more professional approach to accreditation. One of the difficulties surrounding the old system was the reliance on volunteer input from assessors. The new system allows for dedicated staff to work closely together to agreed deadlines ensuring that all applications receive a more standardised assessment from a group of people trained and experienced in a variety of therapeutic approaches. Only time will tell what real advantages or disadvantages the new system will bring.

From 1 April 2000, BACP introduced changes which affected the accreditation categories. Members were placed in two categories: those of 'registered' or 'senior registered' practitioners. The 'grand-parenting' scheme became available for a limited period of time (to 31 December 2001) for counsellors, counselling supervisors and trainers who had ten or more years experience prior to 1 April 2000. Applicants wishing to demonstrate how they meet the accreditation criteria for their area of professional practice and a variety of specific transitional tasks were 'road tested' by a group of members to ensure straightforward access as well as equivalence in rigour to the current schemes. Successful completion enabled the candidate to move into BACP's registered practitioner category. BACP ran a series of success-ful regional workshops to assist members understand the accredita-tion process, consider whether the 'grandparenting' scheme was applicable to them and, if not, the steps individuals would be required to take to work towards meeting the accreditation criteria.

One of the biggest changes to the accreditation process applies to the re-accreditation procedures. Currently, re-accreditation is required every five years and the counsellor has to be able to demonstrate an existing practice of 150 hours a year. Under the new scheme a counsellor will be able to cease client contact work and be able to keep accredited status by undertaking 30 hours of recognised continued professional development (CPD).

Accreditation continues to become the yardstick by which employers and the general public measure the efficacy of counsellors and their training. Although there is opposition to the accreditation process, it is unlikely to be replaced until either a uniform type of training exists for all counsellors or a more radical educational programme takes place adequately to inform all interested parties. As neither of these options seems viable, it is likely that some form of recognition by professional bodies such as the BACP will continue to be widely accepted.

REFERENCES

British Association for Counselling and Psychotherapy (1999). *Individual accreditation pack*. Rugby: BACP.

Frankland, A. (1997). An invitation to accreditation – steps towards and emerging profession. *Counselling*, 6(1), 55–60.

Gibbon, J. (1990). Accreditation: a personal view. *Counselling*, 1(2), 39.

Mowbray, R. (1995). *The case against psychotherapy registration*. London: Trans Marginal Press.

Schapira, S.K. (2000). *Choosing a counselling or psychotherapy training*. London: Routledge.

Totton, N. (1997). The Independent Practitioners Network: a new model of accountability. In R. House & N. Totton (Eds), *Implausible Professions*. Ross-on-Wye: PCCS Books.

Wilkins, P., & Frankland A. (1997). *Professional recognition: accreditation and re-accreditation*. Rugby: BACP.

3

United Kingdom Council for Psychotherapy (UKCP)

Kasia Szymanska and Stephen Palmer

The United Kingdom Council for Psychotherapy (UKCP) is a national umbrella organisation for psychotherapies. Its organisational aim is to promote the profession of psychotherapy within the UK to the highest of standards. The organisation consists of 80 member organisations, which are grouped according to eight sections. These sections represent theoretical approaches to psychotherapy, such as analytical psychotherapy and behavioural and cognitive psychotherapy.

THE UKCP'S DEVELOPMENT

The UKCP was initially known as the United Kingdom Standing Conference for Psychotherapy (UKSCP) when it was founded in 1989. It was developed as a result of government pressure to regulate the practice of psychotherapy. Prior to 1989 any member of the public with or without training could call themselves a psychotherapist and practise psychotherapy, despite earlier moves to remedy this situation; for example, the Private Member's Bill put forward by an MP in 1981 to regulate psychotherapy, which failed at its second reading in the House of Commons. In 1993 when a register of psychotherapists was developed, the UKSCP changed its name to the UKCP. The register enabled members of the public looking for psychotherapy to choose a psychotherapist who not only had received adequate training but also abided by a code of ethics.

Seven years on, the UKCP is the UK's largest umbrella body for psychotherapy and has 5000 qualified psychotherapists included on its National Register of Psychotherapists, which is updated on an annual basis.

WHAT IS PSYCHOTHERAPY?

The question as to what is psychotherapy is difficult to answer, as the different sections of the UKCP vary in their definitions and practice of psychotherapy. For example, psychotherapists who are members of the Psychoanalytic and Psychodynamic Section may refer to clients as patients, focus on impact of early experiences on client's current problems, make use of free association, fantasies and transference and may see clients more than once a week. Members of the Behavioural and Cognitive Psychotherapy Section may refer to clients, not patients, focus on the here and now and largely not on the past, tend to favour the application of techniques and self-help to help clients cope with their problems and see clients on a weekly basis.

Bearing in mind the differences in training and practice it would be hard to find a definition that would be acceptable to all the psychotherapists on the UKCP's National Register. However, it is safe to say that psychotherapists work from a non-judgemental and empathic stance to assist their clients in developing insight into their problems in order to help them make appropriate changes in their lives.

THE PSYCHOTHERAPIST

The UKCP produces a biannual publication which all registered psychotherapists receive. This publication contains a variety of information for psychotherapists on issues such as the UKCP's work, the annual conference and contributions from individual psychotherapists and sections. For example, Dr Andrew R. Arthur (2000) outlined a study he undertook which focused on the possible links between theoretical orientation and the personalities of psychotherapists. His participants were drawn from two sections, The Behavioural and Cognitive Section and the British Confederation of Psychotherapists who at the time were a member organisation of the Psychoanalytic and Psychodynamic Section. On the basis of a questionnaire which psychotherapists completed, he concluded that there are differences in personality between psychotherapists who practise within these two orientations. Psychoanalytic psychotherapists are more likely to avoid risks and be aware of anxiety and depression, often using their intuition and imagination to enhance their understanding. Cognitive behaviour therapists are less likely to experience depression or anxiety, to be pragmatic and objective, placing greater value on empiricism. This study is one of the many interesting articles published in the UKCP newsletter, *The Psychotherapist*, which in addition to providing a forum for discussion also enables psychotherapists to keep up to date with the important developments in the psychotherapeutic arena such as the Psychotherapy Bill.

THE PSYCHOTHERAPY BILL

Together with seven other bodies, e.g. the British Psychological Society (BPS), the UKCP is working towards a Psychotherapy Bill, which would result in statutory registration for psychotherapists. This would mean that anyone claiming to be a psychotherapist would by law have to be on a register and abide by a strict code of conduct and ethics. Only psychotherapists who have reached a high level of competence would be included on the register. This Bill is being pushed through parliament because the current procedures adopted to regulate the profession are not adequate. At present, not all psychotherapists are included in the National Register of Psychotherapists. Therefore people looking for psychotherapy may inadvertently be seen by individuals professing to be psychotherapists who in reality have little or no training to help them and may even go on to exploit them financially or sexually. If the client then chooses to complain they may find that the psychotherapist is not a member of any organisation, which means their only option is to take legal action against the psychotherapist. Alternatively, if the psychotherapist belongs to an organisational member of the UKCP, the client can complain to the organisation. If the psychotherapist has breached ethical standards, he may be expelled from the organisation and his name struck off the National Register of Psychotherapists. However, that would not stop him setting up a new practice as psychotherapist without the organisation's permission. Therefore the register would go some way towards protecting the public from unqualified and unscrupulous psychotherapists as any psychotherapist expelled from the register would be prohibited legally from working as a psychotherapist.

SECTIONS OF THE UKCP

The UKCP consists of eight sections, to which are affiliated a number of member organisations and two institutional members and two special members.

The Analytical Section

Analytical psychotherapists work from a Jungian perspective. They aim to help clients understand their inner world or psyche through a journey of self-discovery. Through the experience of psychotherapy, analytical psychotherapists aid clients in their endeavours to articulate the unconscious. A key component of this approach is the analysis of dreams and the relationship between the psychotherapist and client, i.e. the focus on transference and countertransference.

Analytical psychotherapists often work with patients who perceive they lack meaning in their lives, had difficult childhoods, or may have relationship problems.

Member organisations include the Association of Jungian Analysts and Confederation of Analytical Psychologists.

Behavioural and Cognitive Psychotherapy Section

Behavioural and cognitive psychotherapists help clients to modify their feelings and behaviours by challenging their unhelpful ways of thinking. Based on an assessment of the client's problems, behavioural and cognitive psychotherapists work in a collaborative and structured manner with clients to help them manage their problems. They use a wide range of techniques and often give clients homework to do in-between sessions; so a client with a fear of flying may be asked to read about aeroplanes and how they work as a homework assignment.

This psychotherapy is applied to a number of psychological problems such as anxiety, depression, psychosomatic disorders, eating disorders, substance misuse, stress management, chronic fatigue and post traumatic stress disorder (PTSD).

Member organisations include the British Association of Behavioural and Cognitive Psychotherapies (BABCP).

Experiential Constructivist Therapies Section

Psychotherapists in this section focus on the personal meanings or constructs which clients bring to therapy. They help clients to understand the meanings they have attached to their own experiences, to make choices and to explore and experiment with alternatives. Psychotherapists use a number of strategies tailored to the clients' needs in order to bring about changes in behaviour, ideas or value systems. These therapies can be applied to individuals and groups and to problems such as anxiety, depression and stuttering.

Member organisations include the Association for Neuro-linguistic Programming and Centre for Personal Construct Psychology.

Family, Couple, Sexual and Systemic Therapy Section

The member organisations belonging to this section 'share an assumption that individuals' problems cannot adequately be understood without considering the wider relevance of the families and groups which form each individual's past and present wider context' (UKCP website information). Therefore, psychotherapists belonging to this section focus both on past issues and the here and now either on an individual basis, with couples, or with families. For example, psychotherapists practising sex therapy may work with a couple or on a one-to-one basis, helping clients to cope with sexual problems such as impaired sexual interest, orgasmic dysfunction and impotence. Often this type of therapy is relatively short term. On the other hand, family psychotherapists work with two or more individuals addressing the family system, focusing on how changes in one family member can impact on the whole family or system. They may use a variety of techniques such as genograms, which are similar to family trees and constructed by the family in order to understand the evolution of problems and possible triggers.

Member organisations include the British Association for Sexual and Relationship Therapy and Kensington Consultation Centre.

Humanistic and Integrative Psychotherapy Section

This section encompasses four psychotherapies that place emphasis on the integration of the body, feelings, mind and spirit.

The first approach in this section, humanistic psychotherapy, is non-directive, focuses on the here and now and recognises that human beings are creative and trustworthy individuals who strive towards greater self-awareness. The psychotherapist and client do not necessarily work towards goals and there is much emphasis on three core conditions, congruence, unconditional positive regard and empathy.

The second approach, existential psychotherapy, draws on the work of philosophers and is a direct approach that concentrates on the past, present and future. The focus of the psychotherapy is to support the client in making sense of their experience of 'being in the world'.

The third approach, transpersonal/psychospiritual psychotherapy is concerned with helping the client to find their own spiritual path in life. Psychotherapists work with levels of consciousness and like existential psychotherapists focus on the past, present and future to address clients well-being.

The fourth approach, integrative therapy stresses the application of different theories and approaches in order to help the client to deal with their problem(s). The integrative psychotherapist draws on theories which they believe will be of benefit to understanding and helping the client and does not try to view the client's problems from only one theoretical approach.

Member organisations include the Association of Cognitive Analytic Therapists and the Minster Centre.

Hypno-Psychotherapy Section

This approach combines the application of hypnosis and psychotherapy to aid clients in reaching an altered state of awareness/relaxation. This is induced in a collaborative manner by the psychotherapist to help clients access and channel resources from their unconscious mind to resolve problems. Hypno-psychotherapists use a number different of strategies to induce hypnosis and when clients are hypnotised they use appropriate techniques to facilitate change. Hypnosis is primarily carried out within the context of a psychotherapeutic relationship to help clients treat and relieve a variety of problems. These include building confidence, improving sports performance, controlling pain, stopping smoking, eliminating nail biting and coping with insomnia.

Member organisations include the National School of Hypnosis and Psychotherapy and British Autogenic Society.

Psychoanalytic and Psychodynamic Section

Psychoanalytic psychotherapists assume that patients' problems have their origins in childhood experiences. They place emphasis on the unconscious and within the therapeutic relationship work with clients to make the unconscious conscious through the use of free association, interpretation of dreams, transference and countertransference. In many ways their practice is similar to that of the analytical psychotherapists, only the latter work from a Jungian perspective and psychotherapists listed under this section employ mainly Freudian or Kleinian approaches. The psychotherapists tend to see patients over a long period, often twice weekly, or work psychodynamically to provide short-term brief therapy.

Member organisations include the Arbours Association and the Institute of Group Analysis.

Psychoanalytically based Therapy with Children

In this developing area psychoanalytic psychotherapists work with children who often have behavioural or emotional problems. As with adult psychoanalytic therapy the emphasis is on communication and the unconscious, with an additional focus on drawing, play and educational tasks. Often because the child is part of a family system the parents and/or family are also asked to go into treatment.

The two member organisations are the Association of Child Psychotherapists and Forum for the Advancement of Educational Therapy and Therapeutic Teaching.

Institutional members

This category is open to organisations that due to their complexity, size or range of therapeutic approaches practised do not subscribe to the individual sections. The two organisations are the Tavistock Clinic and Universities Psychotherapy Association.

Special members

The two organisations in this section, the British Psychological Society (see Chapter 4 for more information about the BPS) and the Royal College of Psychiatrists, are deemed special members because they come from allied disciplines which also provide a contribution to psychotherapy as a profession.

Friend of the Council

This category is for the British Association of Counselling and Psychotherapy (see Chapter 2 for more information about BACP).

TRAINING TO BE A PSYCHOTHERAPIST

To become registered with the UKCP all psychotherapists must undergo formal training and become accredited by their own sections before applying for UKCP registration. For example, a psychotherapist practising cognitive behaviour therapy needs to become accredited by the BABCP (see guidelines below) first before registering with the UKCP. The training courses are often run or accredited by the member organisations, not the UKCP. Although the UKCP does stipulate that all the member organisations run or accredit training courses at postgraduate level for individuals with suitable personal qualities, some prior experience of working with people, and that the course must be approximately of four years duration part time, the content of the training varies, depending on the requirement of the member organisations.

As psychotherapy training takes some years to complete, it is important to join a course with some prior knowledge of the therapeutic approach or orientation being taught. Initially, attendance of short introductory courses that focus on one or more approaches may be beneficial, as many people are not suited to all models of therapy. To discover that you do not like a particular approach after enrolment can be expensive and time-consuming. Chapter 5 covers the main theoretical approaches that may be helpful. Introductory texts on therapy may also assist a prospective trainee in the selection of a specific orientation. *Introduction to Counselling and Psychotherapy* (Palmer, 2000) includes 23 approaches to therapy and provides case examples with each one.

A COMPARISON OF ACCREDITATION PROCEDURES BETWEEN TWO MEMBER ORGANISATIONS

Registration as a psychotherapist via the BABCP route

In order for individuals to become accredited by the BABCP, they need to fulfil the following criteria:

- Have completed a psychology degree plus an applied qualification or professional training in a specific area such as nursing, medicine, education, counselling, occupational therapy, probation or social work.
- Have completed two years of professional practice in their chosen profession, e.g. social work.
- Are able to show evidence of good practice, e.g. have experience of providing therapy to clients using cognitive and/or behavioural theory (CBT) and show an understanding of the therapeutic relationship. Evidence will be assessed on the basis of a competent supervisor's report.
- Indicate their commitment to theory and practice for at least the last two years via attendance on courses, workshops, reading relevant CBT books or journals and conducting research.
- Be in regular supervision provided by other psychotherapists with experience of this approach. The type of supervision may vary from group, individual to telephone supervision. Often in order to enhance clinical effectiveness and ensure ethical standards are met, CBT supervisees audio/video tape their therapy sessions.
- Have received specialised training in cognitive behaviour theory and practice.
- Adhere to the Guidelines for Good Practice of Behavioural and Cognitive Psychotherapy published by the BABCP.

Fulfilment of the above criteria normally leads to accreditation. Individuals can then choose if they wish to be registered with the UKCP.

Registration with the UKCP via the Forum for Independent Psychotherapists (FIP) route

In order for individuals to be accredited by the FIP as an individual psychoanalytic psychotherapist they need to satisfy the following criteria:

- Attend a postgraduate course of approximately 500 hours, which includes theoretical input on, for example, Freud and Klein and understanding and/or experience of, for example, infant development and psychotherapy with clients who are mentally ill.
- Have been in personal therapy for a year prior to the start of training and remain in personal therapy for the duration of their training with a psychoanalytic therapist for approximately twice a week.
- Gain clinical experience over a period of three years.
- Be in regular weekly supervision. While supervisees see a number of clients, they are required to see one client for at least once a week for a period of two years.
- Attend clinical seminars and present their own work.
- Be formally assessed in relation to theoretical understanding and clinical practice.

The FIP also provides accreditation as an individual psychodynamic psychotherapist, which is similar to the above accreditation process.

While both accreditation procedures are rigorous and ultimately lead to the same conclusion – accreditation and then UKCP registration – there are differences in the training processes. One major difference is the requirement for personal therapy. The BABCP does not require trainees to be in personal therapy, although many BABCP psychotherapists have been or are in therapy. This stance is taken as there is little research to demonstrate that experience of therapy helps a therapist to become more therapeutically effective. While the FIP states that trainees should be in therapy for one year prior to training and for the duration of training, ultimately this can contribute to rising training costs. A second difference in the training is clinical practice. Cognitive behavioural trainees usually see clients for short-term therapy (six to 12 sessions) plus, while FIP trainees are required to see at least one client for a period of two years.

STRUCTURE OF UKCP

The UKCP is a structured organisation (see Figures 3.1 and 3.2). The governing board and the various committees work together to develop

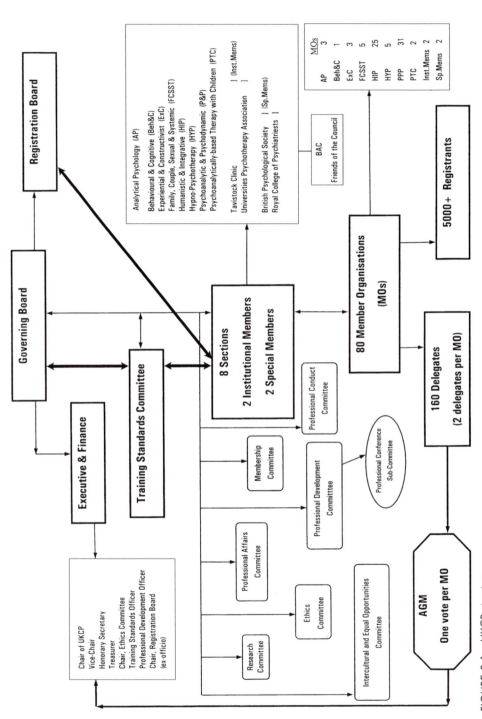

FIGURE 3.1 *UKCP structure*

1   *Governing board.* The Governing Board is composed of 8 Section representatives, 7 Elected Officers, 4 Ordinary Members, 2 Special Member representatives, 2 elected Institutional Member representatives, and the Chair of the Registration Board. Section representatives are appointed by each Section. Elected Members (Officers, Ordinary Members and Institutional Members) are elected at the AGM.

2   *Registration Board.* The Registration Board members are appointed by Sections. Each Section can appoint representatives to the Registration Board in the ratio of one representative for every ten or part thereof approved training or accrediting organisations in that Section. In addition, every Special Member and every Institutional Member appoints a representative. The Registration Board appoints its own Chair at the first meeting of every year.

3   *Training Standards Committee.* Each Section can appoint representatives to the Training Standards Committee in the ratio of one representative for every ten or part thereof approved training or accrediting organisations in that Section. In addition, every Special Member and every Institutional Member appoints a representative to sit on the committee. The Chair of the Training Standards Committee is elected at the AGM.

FIGURE 3.2   *Notes on the UKCP structure*

and enhance the UKCP's profile and ensure that the member organisations maintain high professional standards. Volunteers, who are UKCP registered, usually staff committees. They provide their time freely. This is no different to most other professional organisations.

The Professional Conference Sub-Committee organises the annual conference, while the Continuing Professional Development Committee (CPD) plays a significant role in developing CPD guidelines for psychotherapists. In the spring 2000 issue of *The Psychotherapist*, this committee outlined in an article the discussion with conference delegates on continuing professional development. Questions such as 'What is professional development?' and 'Where does the responsibility for CPD lie?' were addressed and conference delegates' views were taken into account in order that the UKCP produces a cohesive CPD policy to which individual psychotherapists can adhere (UKCP, 2000).

FUTURE OF UKCP

During 2000, the British Association for Counselling became the British Association for Counselling and Psychotherapy (BACP). As the BACP has three times more members than the UKCP, soon it could be viewed as the main umbrella body for psychotherapists. If the United Kingdom Register of Counsellors (UKRC) which is supported by the BACP, decides to include psychotherapists and becomes the United Kingdom Register of Counsellors and Psychotherapists (UKRCP), the status of the UKCP could be challenged. In addition, the British Psychological Society is setting up its own Register of Psychotherapists who will be qualified psychologists with training specific to psychotherapy.

It is worth mentioning the British Confederation of Psychotherapists (BCP), an analytical based organisation that takes an exclusive approach to membership; i.e. its organisational members are not permitted membership of other bodies such as the UKCP. In contrast to this, the UKCP has a more open policy to dual membership. Historically, the BCP split from the former UKCP (UKSCP) in 1992. Thus, instead of diverse psychotherapy organisations working together towards common goals, there have been on going tensions for some years.

With the potential changes to the UKRC, the development of the BPS register, and the ongoing difficult relationship with the BCP, fewer psychotherapists may wish to become UKCP registered. This could have a knock-on effect and reduce the UKCP revenue and influence. However, taking a positive view, it is likely that most of the registers will flourish, as they will be offering different facilities to their members. Paradoxically, the exclusive inward-looking policy of the BCP is potentially self-limiting.

REFERENCES

Arthur, A.R. (2000). Do I choose my orientation: or does it choose me? *The Psychotherapist*, 4, 24.

Palmer, S. (2000). *Introduction to counselling and psychotherapy: the essential guide*. London: Sage.

UKCP (2000). Continuing professional development: feedback from the UKCP AGM 70-9 January parallel session. *The Psychotherapist*, 4, 8.

4

British Psychological Society (BPS)

Jill D. Wilkinson

Counselling psychology is still a relatively young branch of applied professional psychology with the first trainees graduating from a BPS recognised training route in counselling psychology in 1997. More recently, the BPS has been developing procedures for the recognition of psychotherapists within the BPS. This chapter will examine and explore routes to becoming a chartered counselling psychologist and a BPS recognised psychotherapist.

BECOMING A CHARTERED COUNSELLING PSYCHOLOGIST

Prerequisite criteria

Before beginning training as a chartered counselling psychologist it is necessary to have been granted the Graduate Basis for Registration (GBR) of the British Psychological Society. Eligibility for the GBR can be obtained by successfully completing one of the following:

- a BPS accredited first degree course in psychology or where psychology is the major component; or, for those overseas students who hold a degree in psychology not recognised by the BPS, by applying directly to the Admissions Committee of the BPS, which deals with applications on an individual basis.

- the qualifying examination of the BPS which is intended for people who are graduates, but who do not hold an honours degree in psychology recognised by the Society and who are therefore not yet eligible for GBR.

- a BPS accredited conversion course in psychology which is similarly intended for people who are graduates, but who do not hold an honours degree in psychology recognised by the Society.

Having gained the GBR, there are several routes, outlined below, to becoming a chartered counselling psychologist:

- By the gaining the BPS Diploma in Counselling Psychology (the professional qualifying examination in counselling psychology) after a period of approved independent study and practice. This is sometimes referred to as the 'Independent Route'.

- By successfully completing a postgraduate course accredited by the BPS which will lead to the award of Statement of Equivalence to the Diploma in Counselling Psychology.

- By a combination of the above.

Additionally, psychologists from other branches of applied psychology who have pursued a course of study and practice in counselling psychology and psychologists who have obtained their qualifications in counselling psychology overseas may apply to the BPS Admissions Committee to be granted chartered counselling psychologist status.

BPS DIPLOMA IN COUNSELLING PSYCHOLOGY (THE INDEPENDENT ROUTE)

The Diploma in Counselling Psychology (subsequently referred to as the Diploma) is awarded after three years full-time (or part-time equivalent) study at postgraduate level. Information about the Diploma can be found in the 'Regulations and Syllabus for the Diploma in Counselling Psychology' (subsequently referred to as the Regulations and Syllabus) available from the BPS. This document is updated every year so prospective candidates should acquaint themselves with the latest edition.

Having enrolled for the Diploma, trainees pursuing the independent route follow a plan of training which they will have designed themselves, on the lines set out in the Regulations and Syllabus, and with the help of a co-ordinator of training (an experienced chartered counselling psychologist) and which will have been approved by the Registrar of the Board of Examiners. It is essential that candidates have their training plans approved by the Registrar, before embarking on their postgraduate training in counselling psychology. It is then the job of the Board of Examiners for the Diploma in Counselling Psychology to examine the candidate's work.

The Diploma is in two parts: Part 1, consisting of five components, is taken over one year full-time, or two years part-time equivalent, and Part 2, with six components, over two years full-time or four years part-time. The various components are examined once a year and candidates choose which components they wish to submit for examination for a given year. The components of the Diploma are as follows:

- *Counselling psychology practice* which should be conducted in more than one setting and comprise at least 150 client-contact hours for Part 1 and 300 client-contact hours for Part 2, with supervision at a ratio specified in the Regulations and Syllabus. This component is assessed by means of client studies, process reports, client logs and supervisors' reports.

- *Counselling psychology skills* which involve the candidate in engaging in a minimum of 80 hours of experiential workshop training for Part 1 of the Diploma and 150 hours for Part 2. This is assessed by an attendance record signed by the co-ordinator of training.

- *Self-reflection and personal development* which includes a require-ment for candidates at Part 1 to undertake at least 40 hours individual personal therapy and a recommendation that candi-dates for Part 2 pursue their individual therapy, although they are not required to do so. Additionally a personal diary must be kept throughout for use as a resource in supervision.

- *Academic competence* as outlined in the Regulations and Syllabus and which includes subjects under the headings of Practical Competence, Ethical and Legal Issues, Self-reflection and Personal Development, Psychological Knowledge and Research and Evaluation. Academic competence in Part 1 is assessed by means of a three-hour seen written paper and in Part by 2 by a three hour seen written paper and a 4000 to 6000 word essay.

- *Research competence* (Part 2 only) which is demonstrated by can-didates undertaking a research project relevant to counselling psychology and submitting a 12,000 to 15,000 word research report for assessment.

- *Overall competence* which refers to the integration of a candidate's academic learning, professional practice, research competence and personal presentation as a colleague. It is expected that overall competence will be demonstrated by the assessment procedures outlined above but candidates may be called for an interview by the Board of Examiners.

It can be seen from the above that there may be a number of issues and questions which may arise for prospective candidates.

How can I find a co-ordinator of training and what should I expect from one?

A co-ordinator of training must be a chartered counselling psychologist with post-qualifying experience. Some counselling psychologists see the role of co-ordinator of training as a major part of their professional practice, while others may not wish to get involved in training at all or take on only the occasional candidate. A list of chartered counselling psychologists is available from the BPS and it is up to the trainee to approach a potential co-ordinator. Most trainees approach someone within travelling distance, but this is by no means essential in the world of electronic communications, and indeed may be impossible for those living in more remote areas. Do not be afraid to ask a prospective co-ordinator about post-qualifying experience, experience of acting as co-ordinator of training, fees, etc. You will also need to be clear about how often you would ideally like to meet with your co-ordinator and the level of support you feel you will need. Will you need help with finding placements, supervisors, writing client studies and process reports? Clearly these are issues which need to be clarified and agreed on before any commitments are made either way. It is also very important that you feel that your co-ordinator of training is a person whom you can both respect and get on with as, under normal circumstances, candidates should work with the same co-ordinator of training for the duration of the Diploma.

How do I gain my counselling psychology practice experience and how do I find an appropriate therapy supervisor?

Most trainees gain their therapeutic experience by either getting jobs as assistant psychologists in NHS psychology departments, community mental health teams, in primary care, or by finding placements in various counselling services, including voluntary agencies.

Being employed as an assistant psychologist clearly has its advantages, apart from financial ones. In such a post, you would be part of a team with opportunity for cross-disciplinary interaction, which is an important part of professional training. You would probably have some opportunity to observe experienced therapists in action, receive in-house supervision, as well as some in-house training and you will be exposed to clients with severe and serious problems and symptoms. However, you need to be aware that you will probably be working within a medical/psychiatric model, and that in the majority of NHS settings the major theoretical orientation is cognitive behavioural.

An alternative approach is to explore possible placements in counselling services, such as those in educational establishments and agency settings (including voluntary agencies) offering, for example, HIV and AIDs counselling, bereavement care or victim support. Here too you may have the opportunity to observe experienced therapists with their clients and receive in-house training. However, you will need to check with the BPS that the supervision offered is acceptable to them. They require that supervisors 'will normally be Chartered Counselling Psychologists with appropriate training or expertise in supervision although other suitably qualified persons will be considered' (Regulations and Syllabus for the Diploma in Counselling Psychology, 1999–2000: 25). If the supervision offered is not acceptable you will need to find out whether the agency or counselling service in question would agree to you having external supervision, for which it would be necessary to pay. You also need to check that you will see a sufficient range of clients to satisfy your training needs and that you will get sufficient psychological input from the organisation.

How do I go about getting my counselling psychology skills training?

Many academic institutions, including several of those running courses accredited by the BPS to confer eligibility for chartered counselling psychologist status, offer modules in areas relevant to the Diploma in Counselling Psychology. There are also a number of part-time courses in specific theoretical orientations, such as psychodynamic or cognitive therapy. In addition, a number of independent organisations offer preparation to candidates for the Diploma. In planning your training, you need to check that courses match the criteria laid down in the Regulations, that they are at the appropriate postgraduate level (usually a diploma for Part 1 and masters for Part 2), and offer an appropriate psychological input into the training. The UKCP issues a training booklet that includes a list of courses and the BACP will provide information about courses which it has accredited. The internet is another source of information about modules and courses, with most educational establishments having their own websites. Training organisations and courses are also often advertised in the BPS journals *Counselling Psychology Review* and *The Psychologist*.

How do I find a therapist?

The Regulations and Syllabus state that the candidate's personal therapist will normally be a chartered counselling psychologist, but that other suitably qualified and experienced therapists will be considered. The BPS can provide a list of chartered counselling psychologists and most psychotherapists on registers of reputable bodies such as the UKCP and the BCP (British Confederation of Psychotherapists) would probably be considered appropriate providers of personal therapy.

In selecting a personal therapist, you need to think carefully about the theoretical orientation of the therapist in relation to your own needs and theoretical orientation. Another consideration is that counselling psychology, although a rapidly expanding field, is still not large. You will therefore need to be careful that you do not find yourself in a position of, for example, being taught or supervised by your therapist and thereby entering into a dual relationship, which would be unacceptable.

How do I go about doing a research project and finding a research supervisor?

Unless you are particularly research orientated, probably the most manageable way of tackling the research component is by attending a suitable research module (and possibly a dissertation module) at one of the higher education institutions. This may also have the benefit of putting you in touch with possible research supervisors (although you may need to pay extra for this). It is, however, important to check that any such module is offered at postgraduate level and that it is relevant to counselling psychology.

Are there any support networks for trainees?

Trainees in various parts of the UK have organised themselves into informal groups to offer mutual support and an opportunity to share information, experience, expertise, etc.

Is the 'Independent Route' for me?

The Independent Route suits people who are highly motivated, self-disciplined and enjoy working independently. If you are considering pursuing this route, you will also need to have good planning, including financial planning, skills. Supervisors, co-ordinators of training, training courses, modules and personal therapists all need paying for, in additions to the Diploma fees. If this sounds a little daunting, you need to bear in mind that the 'independent route', because of its flexibility, offers a marvellous opportunity for you to design a creative, innovative programme of training unique to you.

For a discussion about criteria and standards in relation to the Diploma see Strawbridge (1999). If you want some idea about what might be confronting you, if you are considering the Independent Route, see Bartlett (1999).

ACCREDITED COURSES

A second way to become a chartered counselling psychologist is to undertake a postgraduate training course that has been accredited by the BPS which will enable candidates to be awarded a Statement of Equivalence to the Diploma in Counselling Psychology; thereby conferring eligibility for registration as a chartered psychologist (in addition to gaining the university's own postgraduate award). There are several such courses based in universities or other academic institutions and the BPS will supply an up-to-date list.

The Regulations and Syllabus for the Diploma in Counselling Psychology (devised for those following the Independent Route) form a set of baseline regulations for courses. Most courses offer training that is accredited to be equivalent to both Parts 1 and 2 of the Diploma, but some are accredited only to be equivalent to Part 1.

All accredited courses must incorporate five key elements: theoretical studies; supervised counselling psychology practice; experiential training; personal development training and research. However, there is considerable variation in the core philosophy of courses as well as the structure and content of the training and the level of the award offered by the various institutions.

Each course is required by the BPS to make explicit its core philosophy, including its orientation and values. Some courses may emphasise multicultural practice, some may be geared towards mainstream psychological practice in the NHS, others to agency and counselling settings. Some may specialise in two theoretical orientations, others may provide a wider range. Course prospectuses give some information; another source is the list of interests and publications of those teaching on the course. Indeed, this may give you an even better idea than 'official' documentation.

Some issues and questions that may arise for potential trainees considering this route to chartering are discussed below.

The award – what will I end up with having done a BPS accredited course?

Having successfully completed a BPS accredited course in counselling psychology, you will be awarded the Statement of Equivalence to the Diploma in Counselling Psychology and be eligible for chartered counselling psychologist status. Accredited courses, however, vary considerably in the level of the postgraduate award offered by the institution running the course, with some awarding masters degrees and others postgraduate diplomas for courses accredited to Part 1 of the Diploma. The relation of Part 2 of the Diploma to academic awards is equally confusing and ranges from MSc through Post-MSc Diploma to PsychD (Practitioner Doctorate).

How long is the training?

Some courses are set up in such a way as to encourage trainees to undertake their training over a number of years and offer considerable flexibility in terms of part-time study. Others prefer trainees to complete their training in three years of full-time study, and while offering part-time options, do so only as a fallback position if the candidate is unable to complete his or her training. Both approaches have advantages and limitations. Taking more time allows for the development of the trainee as a therapist, as well as maybe enabling self-funding trainees to work in order to finance their training. One of the advantages of the three-year, full-time route is that it enables the cohort of trainees to stay together for the duration of their training, adding what can be an important supportive dimension to their training.

Is there any funding? What does it cost? What about hidden costs?

Unfortunately, there is no recognised source of funding for counselling psychology training, although some trainees have been successful in obtaining career development loans from banks and small grants from charitable trusts. Another possible source of income is from paid placements, but these tend to be few and far between, and it is only the more experienced trainees, usually either in their final year or those with previous experience, who generally manage to obtain these.

Trainees need to check on the hidden costs of training that may be over and above the fees paid to an institution. These costs may include personal therapy, therapy supervision if it is not offered by the placement, travel to and from placements, library and inter-library loan services, photocopying and computing. Do not hesitate to find out from the respective courses what the fees cover and what costs may be incurred during training.

How do I get my practical therapy experience when attending a course?

Again, courses vary in the way in which placements operate. Some courses have professional tutors, or similar, whose job it is to negotiate and set up placements for their trainees, while other courses provide lists of possible placements for the trainees to negotiate themselves and some courses require trainees to find their own placements.

What previous experience will I need?

Prospective trainees often want to know what previous experience is desirable or necessary before applying for a course. Some courses will and indeed may prefer to take trainees 'from scratch' with no previous direct therapeutic experience or training, while others prefer trainees to have undertaken some counselling training and to have had some experience in therapeutic contexts prior to embarking on their counselling psychology training. The various courses will advise trainees in this respect.

How many trainees would I expect to find on a course? What about staff/trainee ratios?

Some courses have a relatively low intake of trainees per year, around 12, and others offer a greater number of places, particularly those that encourage part-time trainees. Although the BPS requires adequate staffing and resources, these also vary from course to course. It should be relatively easy to check these out, although not all courses make the distinction between part-time and full-time members of staff.

What support will be available?

Training is inherently stressful. It is useful to find out in advance what sort of formal and informal support the course offers. Most institutions have a system of personal tutors and some courses have peer or tutor-led support groups and 'buddy' systems. Personal therapy, a requirement as part of training, and psychodynamic or other experiential groups can give support, although they can also be challenging for the trainee.

Which course?

Which course(s) you choose to apply for will depend on a number of factors which may relate to values and orientation, yours and those of the course(s), as well as practical considerations such as cost and geographic location. If you can, and if the course runs one, do try to go to an open day of any course you might be considering. Here you will probably get an opportunity to talk to staff and current trainees, as well as get a flavour of the course. You may also want to look in journals such as *Counselling Psychology Review, British Journal of Medical Psychology* and *Counselling Psychology Quarterly* to see which staff and trainees are publishing what. This will give you an idea of the research interests of those involved with the course.

Is a course in counselling psychology the training for me?

There has been some criticism of course-based therapeutic training and one of the key issues is whether the culture of an academic institution can be conducive to therapeutic endeavour and personal development. Another issue is that course staff are likely to be involved with both training and assessment of trainees and this can have implications in terms of openness and trust for the trainees. At the same time, course-based training, by virtue of the links between training and assessment, can use assessment constructively, as part of training, so that trainees can get detailed feedback on their assessed work. Staff in turn can, through consideration of the trainees' work submitted for assessment, identify the gaps in their own teaching and rectify these as necessary. Training thus becomes an iterative and creative process.

Those undertaking their training in an academic institution can gain considerable benefit from being a member of a wider intellectual community. Being a member of a university or part of an academic department can offer trainees a wide range of learning experiences and opportunities in terms of access to, for example, seminars, research supervisors from a range of sub-sections in psychology and computing, audio-visual and library facilities. Try to get a feel of the degree to which the course is integrated into the department in which it is run and what seminars and activities other than those offered by the course are available to trainees. For a discussion of ideas related to running a course, see Wilkinson, Campbell, Coyle, Jordan & Milton (1997).

A COMBINED ROUTE

Because both the Independent Route via the Diploma in Counselling Psychology and most accredited courses are organised and offered at Part 1 and Part 2 levels, it is possible to achieve chartered counselling psychologist status by a combination the independent and course-based routes.

The combined route is increasingly popular with trainees, particularly starting with a course accredited to Part 1 and taking Part 2 independently. This enables trainees to gain some therapeutic experience, to find their way around the system and to identify what interests them before embarking on planning and undertaking Part 2 of their training independently.

THE CHALLENGE OF COUNSELLING PSYCHOLOGY TRAINING

Finally come the question: 'Is counselling psychology training and ultimately a career in therapy for me?' As someone who has found working as a counselling psychologist enormously intellectually stimulating and personally rewarding, I would like to encourage all who are interested to explore this as a professional endeavour. However, both at a personal level as a practising therapist and as a trainer of counselling psychologists and a former course director, I am only too aware of the stresses and strains of such a training and of such a profession. Working as we do, we are or will inevitably be confronted by some material that would distress most people, but also material which, because of our own personal histories, is particularly distressing to us and with which we will be required to 'cope'; not by cutting off, not by engaging in denial, but by confronting things in ourselves which may be distressing and even frightening for us. While doing this, we will need to maintain 'real' and genuine therapeutic relationships with our clients – clients with severe symptomatology, as well as very severe life issues and crises. This is just one of the reasons why there is so much emphasis on personal therapy and personal development in counselling psychology and one of the reasons why we need to develop good social and supportive networks.

But what other academic discipline and profession (for counselling psychology is both of these) offers so much in terms of the wealth and richness of the material with which we are working? We are striving to negotiate and understand with our clients how and why they, in particular, are experiencing this difficulty, problem, or particular symptom, in this particular way at this particular time, and to work out ways to alleviate their distress and to help them to move forward in their lives. We are drawing on a wide range of theory, knowledge, practice and research from a number of disciplines and sub-disciplines, and we need always to remain 'in contact' with our clients and ourselves. Challenging, baffling, it often is; frustrating and daunting it sometimes is – boring, never.

THE REGISTRATION OF PSYCHOLOGISTS
SPECIALISING IN PSYCHOTHERAPY

During the 1990s there was considerable discussion about whether there was a need for a BPS register of psychotherapists or whether psychologists trained in psychotherapy should apply to register with, for example, the UKCP. It was decided to take the first of these courses of action, and in the latter part of the 1990s the Standing Committee of Psychotherapy (SCP) of the BPS made considerable progress towards developing standards for accreditation of psychologists.

Considerable debate surrounded what constituted psychotherapy and psychotherapeutic practice, but standards for psychotherapy training for a number of key approaches have now been defined. These approaches include both single, referred to as *formal model approaches*, such as cognitive behavioural psychotherapy and systemic psychotherapy, and multi-model, referred to as *generic approaches*, of the kind often practised by counselling and clinical psychologists.

It is expected that this work will continue and it is envisaged that a sub-register to the Register of Chartered Psychologists will be established to record names of those psychologists achieving BPS standards for accreditation psychotherapy. Psychologists will be accredited at either a practitioner or specialist (consultant) level and it is expected that although the majority of psychologists coming forward for recognition will be either counselling or clinical psychologists, whose training may make them eligible for practitioner level status, the psychotherapy route will be open to all chartered psychologists. Psychologists interested in finding out more about the accreditation of psychologists specialising in psychotherapy should look out for news in *The Psychologist* (the journal of the BPS) or contact the BPS directly.

REFERENCES

Bartlett, S. (1999). The Diploma in Counselling Psychology by the independent route: thoughts from a candidate in free-fall. *Counselling Psychology Review*, 14(4), 190–221.

Strawbridge, S. (1999). Senior Examiner's Report of the 1999 examinations for the Society's Diploma in Counselling Psychology. *Counselling Psychology Review*, 14(4), 190–221.

Wilkinson, J.D., Campbell, E.A., Coyle, A., Jordan, R., & Milton, M. (1997). Trials, tribulations and tentative triumphs: the first three years of a doctorate in counselling psychology. *Counselling Psychology Review*, 12(2), 79–89.

5

Three Main Models of Psychological Counselling

Linda Papadopoulos and Justin Parker

As most students embarking on their professional training quickly realise, there are literally hundreds of different psychotherapeutic approaches described in the literature. The task of going about learning and gaining confidence in using a particular approach can be daunting, especially in the early stages of their career where one may rely more on theoretical descriptions rather than on practical applications and experience of different models. The proliferation of different counselling and psychotherapy theories over the past eight decades has meant that there is no single dominant therapeutic model to help conceptualise and treat psychological problems, but rather a range to choose from. This chapter introduces you to the most widely adopted psychotherapeutic approaches. The commonalties and differences are highlighted between the various approaches and a practical perspective on the usefulness of each approach is also given. Each approach brings a unique perspective to ideas about psychopathology, treatment and specific interventions. Some readers will find that their understanding of different therapeutic approaches will be discussed when interviewed for postgraduate courses, during training and clinical practice. Therefore it is helpful to have a broad foundation with which to guide further independent reading. When evaluating approaches, you should consider the appropriateness of each to particular client groups and problem types.

PSYCHOANALYTIC THERAPY

Psychoanalytic theory, based on Sigmund Freud's (1856–1939) work, emerged during the Victorian period which was characterised by a repressed view of sexuality. Modern views may no longer reflect those attitudes and consequently many of the traditional theories, para-digms and treatments proposed by Freud are seen by some to be culturally inappropriate. However, psychoanalytic theory has evolved throughout the last century with recent proponents integrating classic theoretical concepts with contemporary notions of psychopathology.

Psychoanalysis originated as one of the first 'talking therapies' and has come to serve as a foundation for general theory in counselling and psychology. It is based on the assumption that an inability to mediate between unconscious drives and conscious demands can lead to personality fragmentation and psychological difficulties. Freud's views still have an impact upon contemporary practice, and his reference to defence mechanisms such as denial and repression have become commonplace in our everyday language.

History

Psychoanalytic therapy revolutionised the way that emotional disturbance and psychopathology were viewed. Although he had a medical background, Freud rejected the notion that psychopathology was caused solely by physical malfunctions and focused on the internal workings of the mind or psyche. While exploring the under-lying causes of behaviour, Freud developed the idea of the uncon-scious mind, which he described in his works, *The Interpretation of Dreams* (1900) and *The Psychopathology of Everyday Life* (1901) among others. As well as the works of Freud, those working alongside him such as Carl Jung, Alfred Adler and Hans Sachs also made important contributions to psychoanalytic theory. This was an exciting time in psychology, for it was during this period that psychology began to separate from philosophy and become an independent discipline. For the first time, it came to be acknowledged that psychological disturbance could be treated through the communication of thoughts and ideas.

During World War II, when many of Freud's followers left Europe for the USA, Melanie Klein, Eric Fromm and Erik Erikson, who became known as the neo-Freudians, further developed psycho-analytic theory. They extended the existing theory by adding the concepts of culture and society as well as the development of inter-personal relationships. Today, psychoanalytically trained therapists have expanded the Freudian and neo-Freudian approaches to develop a focus on the importance of 'insight' on the client's ability to reintegrate their personality (Fine, 1973). More recently, contemporary psychoanalysts (Bacal, 1995; Josephs, 1994; Kohut, 1995) have also recognised the communication of empathy as an integral part of the therapeutic process.

Theoretical concepts

Psychoanalytic therapy has been described as human nature seen from the vantage point of conflict (Kris, 1950). Conflict is seen to exist between the conscious and unconscious mind, as well as between biological needs and social demands. The psyche is viewed as dynamic, with an opposing dualism between the conscious and unconscious mind. It is through these conflicts, through the need to seek pleasure and avoid pain, to strike a balance between internal biological motivators and external sociological mediators, that personality develops. This came to be known as the 'Pleasure Principle' (Freud, 1911). Although this principle operates throughout life, it is most prominent in the early years, which Freud believed to be the most formative with regard to our personality.

The psychoanalytic theory of personality views human nature as deterministic, governed by irrational motivations, unconscious forces and instinctual drives. According to this theory, emotional states/ disturbance do not occur randomly, but rather result from previous experiences that have affected the personality development of the individual. Personality is thought to consist of three structures: the *id*, *ego* and *superego*. The id is present at birth and contains all the instinctual and biological drives. A main function of the id is to fulfil the pleasure principle; the demands of the id are largely unconscious. The ego is the part of the personality that has contact with the outer world; it is our social conscious and acts as a mediator between the id and the superego. Unlike the id, it is not present at birth but develops as we mature and through social and environmental interaction. The ego is ruled by the reality principle and its function is to regulate and censor the personality. The superego is the part of the personality that is developed through socialisation rather than through biology. It is especially influenced by relationships with parents and exists largely in the conscious part of the mind. The superego is responsible for enforcing a 'moral code' on the personality. It strives for perfection rather than pleasure and in a sense emulates and eventually takes over parental standards and authority.

The id, ego and superego are all implicated in the development of the personality through the psychosexual stages described by Freud. According to Freud, infants receive gratification through different parts of their body as they develop and grow. These include the oral, anal, phallic and genital stages. According to psychoanalytic theory, an inability to resolve conflict during any one these stages leads to specific personality types which may become problematic as the individual develops. According to Freud, such behaviour is derived from the nature of the parents' involvement with the child at the relevant stage. For example, parents who are overly involved in their child's toilet training can reinforce the importance of the child's toilet behaviours and through this send a message to the child that they must be disciplined. As a consequence we have come to use the term 'anally retentive' to describe people who are obsessively clean and neat.

Therapeutic process

The central aim of the therapeutic process is to help the client understand the ego, to strengthen it and to uncover personality conflicts by making the unconscious conscious. Assessment of the client includes both medical and psychological history-taking in order to identify what symptoms the patient needs to relieve. The biomedical model forms the basis of the conception of pathology and symptoms are viewed as indicators of this. As such, treatment helps to alleviate these symptoms by addressing their source. Through the assessment, hypotheses are developed about the cause of the client's distress. However, these remain undefined until a detailed exploration of the client's unconscious process is undertaken. Following the assessment, early sessions of the therapeutic process are likely to include techniques that will allow the therapist to gain access to the patient's unconscious, such as free association and dream interpretation.

Through an understanding of the client's unconscious, the analyst is able to facilitate the client's conscious awareness of the relationship between their current difficulties and their childhood experiences. Just prior to this realisation, the client's relationship with the therapist becomes the central theme in therapy. This is known as *transference* whereby the client unconsciously begins to relate to the analyst or therapist, who has now become a significant figure in the client's life, in the same way that they have related to a significant other in the past, such as a parent or sibling.

At this stage the analyst's role is to nurture the client's awareness of this unconscious process in particular. However, the analyst must be aware that they themselves may be prone to *countertransference*, whereby unresolved feelings that the therapist has are projected onto the client. Resolution is achieved when both client and therapist feel that these conflicts have been addressed.

Treatment is aimed at reorganising the personality so that the client's superego is able to accommodate those drives, dictated by the id, which have previously been unacceptable. Through this a person is able to maintain an awareness of their needs while negotiating and reaching a balance between those needs and the demands of the outside world.

Limitations

One of the major limitations of this approach is the length of time required to complete a full course of therapy. This also has implications for resources and costs that may make it prohibitive for many people. The approach does not easily lend itself to those seeking practical skills to help them cope with their problems, or indeed those wanting a focused solution-based form of therapy. Although it has long been used to treat marital, sexual and grief-related problems, many of these areas have recently been shown to be more effectively addressed via other therapeutic approaches such as systemic and cognitive therapy (Gilliand & James, 1998). Furthermore, psychoanalytic theory has been criticised for failing to provide evidence of its efficacy and means of testing. As such, scientific validity of this approach has come under scrutiny and remains largely untested. Overall the approach is considered to be effective with clients who require self-exploration or a stabilising therapeutic relationship to address personality and attachment problems. It still remains a widely used and respected therapeutic approach that will undoubtedly continue to influence counselling and psychology for years to come.

COGNITIVE BEHAVIOURAL THERAPY

Cognitive behavioural therapy (CBT) is based on the assumption that the way we perceive events largely determines how we feel about them and in turn how we behave. The therapeutic relationship is collaborative and involves investigating, testing and evaluating clients' beliefs and assumptions. Through this, clients are encouraged to adopt more adaptive beliefs that in turn lead to therapeutic change. The model is largely based upon scientific method whereby a theory must be testable and, as such, refutable. The client's difficulties are viewed as resulting from theories that do not allow them to formulate a correct understanding of their environment (maladaptive). The aim of cognitive interventions is to test the validity of the client's theories (assumptions or schemata) within a collaborative therapeutic relationship. Testing can either address the content of the client's assumptions, by examining the evidence that they collect in their everyday life, or the process by which they come to these assumptions, by engaging in debate about the validity of their reasoning with the therapist. CBT has proven to be very successful, especially in the treatment of anxiety disorders, phobias and depression (Hawton, Salkovskis, Kirk & Clarke, 1994). With the recent advancement of theory to encompass a stronger focus on the client–therapist interpersonal relationship and to incorporate the notion of higher level meta-cognitions as well as negative/irrational beliefs, the theory is moving from strength to strength and remains one of the mainstays of the therapeutic world.

History

The foundations of CBT can be traced back to learning theory and the work of Pavlov on classical conditioning, and later onto the work of Skinner and his insights into operant conditioning. Contemporary CBT theory began in the 1960s with the work of Albert Ellis, considered to be the grandparent of CBT, and Aaron Beck, largely credited with developing ideas for the practice of CBT. While both Ellis and Beck believed that people's underlying assumptions are at the core of their problems, and that active dialogues as opposed to passive listening were vital for the therapeutic process, their approach to clients was different.

Ellis attempted to persuade clients through a didactic approach that their thoughts were unhelpful or irrational. In contrast, Beck adopted active Socratic questioning with clients, allowing them to test and verify the validity of their assumptions. The work of several other behavioural psychologists, such as Bandura's (1977) research on expectancy reinforcements and Mahoney's (1974) work on the cognitive control of behaviour, also influenced cognitive behavioural theory. More recently the work of Meichenbaum on cognitive behavioural modification and Safran's (1990) work on interpersonal process and the cognitive model have further developed the CBT approach.

Theoretical concepts

Cognitive therapy is based on the view that our perceptions of events rather than events themselves cause us to feel and behave in particular ways. Cognitive behavioural theory implies that we learn how to perceive things irrationally or negatively through experiences. These perceptions are usually acquired following a salient life event which evoked a strong emotional reaction; for example, a fear of dogs may originate in a childhood incident where a vicious dog attacks the child. Instead of avoiding that particular dog, the child generalises the feared reaction to all dogs. The individual subsequently generalises the same thoughts and perceptions to all similar events and experiences. A cognitive bias is established and the individual develops a tendency to view and interact with their environment in a negative and irrational way. Systematic errors in reasoning otherwise known as cognitive distortions include the following:

- over-generalisation – when a general assumption is based upon a single event;

- arbitrary inference – coming to conclusions without evidence;
- polarised thinking – interpreting events in an all-or-nothing way;
- personalisation – attributing responsibility for an event only to oneself.

These variants on negative thinking can lead to a vicious cycle where the individual acts in a way that reinforces these unhelpful beliefs. For example, someone who is anxious about public speaking is likely to avoid doing the necessary preparation, and in turn his or her performance may be poorer. This will in turn reinforce their perception of themselves as being a poor public speaker. This applies to various psychological problems including anxiety depression as well as obsessive-compulsive disorder. In many cases, avoidance is considered to be a significant maintaining factor in psychopathology, since the patient is never allowed to challenge their negative or unhelpful thinking and therefore remains unable to overcome their problem.

Therapeutic process

Therapy is aimed at alleviating the clients' symptoms by addressing their maladaptive thoughts, emotional consequences and maintaining behaviours. The scientific method acts as a template for the therapeutic process, whereby clients are encouraged to test their assumptions using evidence they gain in the everyday life.

The purpose of assessment is to define the problem in terms of specific symptoms which cause difficulty, identifying related phenomena such as corresponding cognitions, behaviours, physiological reactions and emotions, and discovering potential 'triggers' in the environment which evoke the undesirable response. Therapists also look at the client's ability to engage in a collaborative relationship based upon challenging unrealistic perceptions.

The therapist's first task is to establish rapport with the client based upon the premise of a collaborative exchange, where the client is explicitly encouraged to take an active role in addressing their difficulty. Treatment may involve 'guided discovery' to identify themes of misinterpretation (i.e. cognitive bias), to challenge maladaptive assumptions and to establish new assumptions which more accurately reflect their environment, as well as develop strategies to help manage situations or symptoms which are identified as causing difficulty.

Therapy sessions are viewed as an opportunity to challenge the client's 'dysfunctional assumptions' about their life or a particular event. The therapist can present challenges within the session either in the form of 'reasoned debate' with the client, through direct training and/or by imagined exposure to the situation. Between sessions, the client is set 'homework' tasks which may involve using opportunities within their 'everyday life' to test the validity of their assumptions, particularly by addressing avoidance, or practising techniques taught during the session.

Progress is monitored throughout treatment and the goals may be redefined if changes do not occur at the rate expected. The success of treatment is evaluated in a number of ways, all of which are either based upon objective measures such as standardised psychometric tests, behavioural change or physiological indicators, or on subjective measures such as self-report or soliciting the views of family or friends, with the client's permission. Subjective measures for change are usually agreed upon, prior to beginning treatment and are the outcome of negotiation of realistic goals obtainable in a given time frame.

Limitations

The theoretical foundations of CBT are based on scientific method and as such a number of criteria are necessary for treatment to be properly carried out. The problem must be defined specifically and expected changes must be 'quantifiable' in some way and must be able to be described by an observable phenomenon, such as behavioural indicators or symptoms intensity. The client must be motivated for change and be able to engage in a collaborative relationship. Similarly, the client needs to have the necessary capacity to process information to identify problem areas. They need to be motivated to accept and implement change, and for this reason assessment of motivation is a crucial part of the therapeutic process. In situations where the limitations of the cognitive approach prevent successful treatment, behavioural interventions may encourage motivation, e.g. token economies, and unreflected changes in behaviour, through 'shaping'. This, however, does not guarantee changes in cognitions, which may remain static (Beck, Rush, Shaw & Emery, 1979).

HUMANISTIC THERAPY

A central tenet of humanistic therapy is that all individuals are resourceful, trustworthy and capable of self-growth and self-understanding. By creating a climate in which there is empathy, genuineness and unconditional positive regard, the client should be able to acknowledge discrepancies between who they are and who they want to be. The approach highlights the client's perception of themself and focuses on their ability to discover new and different ways to understand their reality.

Humanistic therapy was essentially formulated by Carl Rogers (1902–1987). He emphasised that individuals have within themselves vast resources for self-understanding and for altering their self-concepts, behaviours and attitudes toward others. These resources become operative in a definable, facilitative, psychological climate. A therapist who is empathic, caring and genuine creates this climate. Two frequent results of successful humanistic therapy are increased self-esteem and greater openness to experience. To its credit, humanistic therapy allows for diversity and does not foster practitioners who become mere followers of a guru. Counsellors can be person centred and may practise in different ways so long as they demonstrate a belief in the core therapeutic conditions.

The trust in the perceptions and the self-directive capacities of clients expanded client-centred therapy into a person-centred approach to educational group processes, organisational development and conflict resolution. However, economic realities increasingly constrain the client and the practitioner within the field of psychotherapy and the mental health services. These increase the power of systems, institutions and impersonally determined criteria and reduce the importance of individuals, feelings and experience. In one way this weakens the person-centred approach, but in another it ensures its continued existence and growth as a scientifically based system promoting individual worth.

History

Formulated by the psychologist Carl R. Rogers in 1940, humanistic or person-centred therapy is an approach to helping individuals and groups in conflict. It prompted a prolific research based on the revolutionary hypothesis that a self-directed growth process would follow the provision and reception of a particular kind of relationship characterised by genuineness, non-judgemental caring and empathy. In the 1960s and 1970s there was growing interest among counsellors in a 'third force' in therapy as an alternative to the psychoanalytical and behavioural approaches and the person-centred approach fell into this category. Rogers' basic assumptions are that people are essentially trustworthy, that they are capable of self-directed growth if they are involved in a therapeutic relationship. From the beginning he emphasised the personal characteristics and attitudes of the therapist and the quality of client–therapist relationship as the crucial determinants of the outcome of the therapeutic process. Rogers created a furore when he challenged the basic view that the 'counsellor always knows best' and he further challenged the validity of commonly accepted therapeutic procedures such as advice, suggestion, direction, persuasion, teaching, diagnosis and interpretation – many of which have their origins in medical consultations.

In addition to Rogers, Abraham Maslow was instrumental in developing the humanistic trend in psychology. Maslow (1968) focused much of his research on the nature of the self-actualising person and was critical of the Freudian preoccupation with human pathology. Maslow felt that basing findings on a sick population would lead to a form of 'sick psychology' and his belief that the individual has an inherent capacity to move away from maladjustment toward psychological health represents a more positive conceptualisation of human nature.

Theoretical concepts

Perhaps the most fundamental and persuasive concept in humanistic therapy is trust. The foundation of Rogers' approach is an *actualising tendency* present in every living organism. In human beings this tendency refers to one's ability to realise full potential, with regard to relationships, self-esteem and future goals.

Rogers (1980) described the actualising force as part of a tendency toward complexity and greater order. This tendency is present in all things from the simplest of micro-organisms to the complexity of the human mind. Rogers maintained that three particular therapist attributes create a growth-promoting climate in which individuals can move forward and become what they are capable of becoming. These attributes are congruence (or genuineness), unconditional positive regard (acceptance and caring) and accurate empathic understanding (an ability deeply to grasp the subject world of another person). The person-centred approach focuses on clients' responsibility and capacity to discover ways to more fully encounter reality.

The therapeutic process

The goals of person-centred therapy differ from those of traditional psychotherapy approaches. The person-centred approach aims to help the individual attain a greater level of independence and integration. The focus is on the person and not on the person's presenting problem. Rogers (1961) describes people who become increasingly actualised as having an openness to experience, a trust in themselves, an internal source of evaluation and a willingness to continue growing. Encouraging these characteristics is the fundamental goal of humanistic therapy. The role of the therapist is rooted in their ways of being and attitude, not to specific techniques designed to make the client 'do something'.

The therapists utilise themselves as instruments of change where their 'role' is to be effectively without a role. Therapeutic change depends as much on the clients' perception of both their own experience in therapy and of the counsellor's basic attitudes. As counselling progresses, clients are able to explore a wider range of feelings. They can express their fears, anxiety, shame, guilt, anger, hatred and other emotions that they had deemed too negative to incorporate into their self-structure. Increasingly they discover aspects within themselves that they had kept hidden and come to appreciate themselves more as they are, while their behaviour shows more flexibility and creativity.

Rogers (1987) stated that the following six conditions are necessary and sufficient for personality changes to occur:

1   The two individuals are in psychological contact.
2   The 'client' is experiencing incongruency.
3   The therapist is congruent or integrated with respect to the relationship.
4   The therapist experiences unconditional positive regard or real acceptance for the client.
5   The therapist also experiences an empathic understanding of the client's internal reference frame and seeks to communicate this experience to the client.
6   The communication of the therapist's empathic understanding and unconditional positive regard is achieved to a minimal degree.

Rogers asserts that when the therapist can grasp the client's private world in the same way that the client understands it, while maintaining their own separate identity, constructive change is likely to occur.

Limitations

It has been noted that some practitioners have a tendency to be supportive without being challenging and the possibility exists that person-centred therapy will be reduced to an ineffectual therapeutic relationship. It has further been criticised for being overly simplistic and the existence of a growth potential or actualising tendency has been disputed. There is no way to adequately assess whether all people have an actualising tendency within their personality. As such one can never be certain that the core conditions described by Rogers serve the purpose for which they were devised. In terms of training, it has been suggested that more emphasis be placed on helping trainees develop core skills and techniques, rather than focusing so strongly on the personal qualities of the helper.

CONCLUSION

As a trainee therapist embarking on a career in the mental health field, there may be several factors which may encourage you to align yourself with a core therapeutic model. This may be personal choice, the orientation of the course or pure curiosity. However, as indicated by the discussion above, there is no all-encompassing theory to account for the wide variety of difficulties, personalities and situations that one is confronted with when doing therapy. Therefore, therapists need to be aware of the limitations of their chosen approach and also be flexible enough to adopt or refer clients to practitioners practising other theoretical perspectives when these are more appropriate. More importantly, you should also be aware that theory-driven therapies which impose a clearly defined structure upon the client's experience may limit the degree to which the therapist can access the client's 'story'.

For example, a practitioner working within a cognitive behavioural model may find difficulties addressing issues associated with childhood sexual abuse. This may result from an incongruence between the need to adhere to a rigid and structured model and the need to provide the client with the opportunity to define and address their difficulties at a comfortable pace. It is therefore important that you consider the compatibility between the approach used, client groups and problem types.

The common denominator between all of these approaches is their intent to help people, to help them think, feel, behave and relate differently. Each approach described attempts this in a different way based on a different view of personality and psychopathology. No one is necessarily better than the other; rather each has its strengths and weakness. Understanding the origin and rationale upon which each of these is based will allow one to make a judgement not only regarding the model's theoretical appropriateness but its practical efficacy.

As theories develop, the core concepts that the approaches share become more apparent. With training and experience, you should become aware of those concepts and interventions which are compatible and those which are conflictual, particularly with regard to their underlying assumptions. For example, attempting to integrate theoretical perspectives of classical psychoanalysis and staunch behaviourism will be impeded by fundamental differences in core assumptions. As such, you should be able to apply the best of different orientations to create a more inclusive theoretical position to maximise treatment effects. It is likely that at the beginning of your career you will be taught the various counselling approaches as if they are separate, discrete and irreconcilable, as this is the standard way to learn them. However, as you progress in your career, you may find that you adopt an approach where you take what is best from different approaches and match them to what is best for particular clients and do so without subjugating the client's own experience, needs or personality. By doing so, you will be implementing an integrative approach, a topic that you will no doubt encounter frequently as you progress in your training.

As psychological treatments have been increasingly integrated into mainstream healthcare, the efficacy of various treatments has come more and more under scrutiny. Practitioners are required to provide information regarding the success of treatments with respect to different problem types and client groups. This forms the central premise of 'evidence-based practice', where clinical performance is measured against improvements in agreed or established treatment goals. Through this, effective treatments are identified and/or justified. In this way interventions can be targeted at those problems and clients where they produce the best results.

You will find that as a trainee you will be frequently asked to describe and justify the model you work in and how it can be applied in a clinical setting. A clear understanding of an approach can only be achieved by increasing your knowledge base through reading or training courses. Only when you have a firm grasp of the complex ideas and subject matter will you be able to integrate this theory into your practice. Ultimately all models must be complemented by a well-developed reflectivity on the part of the therapist. Without this they remain textbook theories rather than models for positive therapeutic intervention.

REFERENCES

Bacal, H.A. (1995). The essence of Kohut's work and the progress of self psychology. *Psychoanalytic Dialogues, 5*(3), 353–366.

Bandura, A. (1977). Self-efficacy: toward a unifying theory of behavioural change. *Psychological Review, 84*, 191–215.

Beck, A., Rush, A., Shaw, B., & Emery, G. (1979). *Cognitive theory of depression.* New York: Guilford Press.

Fine, R. (1973). Psychoanalysis. In R. Corsini (Ed.), *Current psychotherapies.* Itasca, IL: F.E. Peacock.

Freud, S. (1900). *Complete psychological works of Sigmund Freud (Standard edition volume 4): The interpretation of dreams.* London: Hogarth Press.

Freud, S. (1901). *Complete psychological works of Sigmund Freud (Standard edition volume 6): The psychopathology of everyday life.* London: Hogarth Press.

Freud, S. (1911). *Complete psychological works of Sigmund Freud (Standard edition volume 11): Formulations regarding the two principles of mental functioning.* London: Hogarth Press.

Gilliand, B.E., & James, R.K. (1998). *Theories and strategies in counselling and psychotherapy (4th edn).* London: Allyn & Bacon.

Hawton, K., Salkovskis, P.M., Kirk, J., & Clark, D.M. (1994). *Cognitive behavioural therapy for psychiatric problems: a practical guide*. Oxford: Oxford University Press.

Josephs, L. (1994). Empathic character analysis. *American Journal of Psycho-analysis, 54*(1), 41–54.

Kohut, H. (1995). Introspection, empathy and psychoanalysis: an examination of the relationship between mode of observation and theory. *Journal of Psychotherapy, Practice and Research, 4*(2), 163–167.

Kris, E. (1950). Preconcious mental processes. *Psychoanalytic Quarterly, 19*, 540–560.

Mahoney, M.J. (1974). *Cognition and behaviour modification*. Cambridge, MA: Ballinger.

Maslow, A.H. (1968). *Toward a psychology of being*. Princeton, NJ: Van Nostrand.

Rogers, C.R. (1961). *On becoming a person*. Boston: Houghton Mifflin.

Rogers, C.R. (1980). *A way of being*. Boston: Houghton Mifflin.

Rogers, C.R. (1987). Inside the world of the Soviet professional. *Journal of Humanistic Psychology, 27*, 277–304.

Safran, J.D. (1990). Towards a refinement of cognitive therapy in light of interpersonal theory I: theory. *Clinical Psychology Review, 10*, 87–105.

6

Personal Qualities of a Competent Counsellor

Peter Ruddell and Berni Curwen

A common view exists that the helping professions consist of many people who have been psychologically wounded. A recent study investigated the wounded healer phenomenon among trainee counsellors and found this not to be so (Hanshew, 1998). A further study found that 'personality traits contribute to the prediction of counselor trainee effectiveness . . . trainees who are better adjusted, alert, social, assertive, confident and verbally fluent, tend to be more effective than trainees who appear socially awkward, distant, or who have difficulty establishing relationships' (Williams, 1999). Scragg, Bor & Watts (1999) found that the personality traits of trainee counselling psychologists influenced their preferences for particular models of counselling. In this chapter, we will consider some of the personal qualities which we believe are important for you to become a resourceful and competent counsellor. Counselling itself usually involves aiding others to achieve balance in their lives or in some particular aspects of their lives. Similarly, the counsellor will not necessarily have all of the positive qualities we discuss developed to a high degree but will have a reasonable mix of them.

GENERAL PERSONAL QUALITIES AND COUNSELLING SPECIFIC QUALITIES

The personal qualities of a counsellor might be thought of as divided between general qualities needed to succeed in any venture or profession and personal qualities needed specifically for counselling. For example, if you are disorganised to the extent that you always fail to get to appointments on time, this could present a major problem.

Therefore the ability to manage your time and yourself efficiently and effectively is an important general personal quality for counsellors. If you intend to eventually become a self-employed counsellor, perhaps working at a number of different locations, these qualities will be even more necessary. In this chapter, we will first consider the most general qualities we believe a counsellor requires and move towards those which are more specific to counselling and allied professions. However, the distinction is somewhat arbitrary and therefore some of the qualities we highlight as being particularly germain to counselling may strike you as necessary to other professions too and vice versa.

Two general qualities needed by a counsellor are an adequate level of intelligence and a reasonable memory. Intelligence is involved in a number of the other qualities we go on to discuss in this chapter but aside from these it is necessary for a number of other aspects of counselling. Starting with counselling training, it is necessary for processing all of the material within the course and internalising various components of the chosen model(s) of counselling. These are taken into the counselling sessions (if you progress to this stage) and here you require adequate intelligence to piece together in a comprehensive and meaningful way the sometimes disparate elements of the life of the individual before you. This will sometimes involve you in a form of detective work along with fact-finding missions to fully understand the difficulties facing your client. Here you may sometimes need to be able to add complexity and at other times to simplify a complicated picture. It will also be important to be able to develop a new meaning to fit the 'facts' the client presents on some occasions – a technique known as 'reframing' (Watzlawick, Weakland & Fisch, 1974). A reasonably good memory is needed for this, as well as for remembering the important details of a number of different individuals on your caseload if each is to feel respected by you.

Respect for other individuals is at the heart of counselling and can very quickly be lost if you do not honour a client's confidentiality. While confidentiality is a component which will be covered in counsellor training, and to this extent can be learnt, the counsellor's desire to maintain a client's confidentiality, as well as respecting the individual, both flow from the quality of integrity.

A further general quality which it will be useful for you to have to a reasonable degree if you are to become a counsellor is the ability to work autonomously. At first glance this may seem odd as counselling always involves working with people. However, within the counselling session the counsellor is required constantly to make decisions about interventions and move the therapy in a particular direction. Doing so involves counsellor confidence with the therapy process which itself entails training, intelligence, memory and qualities discussed elsewhere in this chapter. The process also involves developing a working therapeutic relationship with the client and this will also inform the direction that therapy will take at any particular point within a session. Sometimes it will be important to be able to tolerate uncertainty and allow your clients to make their own choices. Conversely you will also need to be able to act decisively and be comfortable acting directively when appropriate. None of this is intended to deny that supervision, which occurs between sessions, can to some extent reduce the degree of autonomy required by the counsellor. Nevertheless, situations occur within the session which demand your ability to make decisions without professional input from others at that time.

Within counselling, counselling psychology and psychotherapy, much emphasis is currently placed on evidence-based practice to ensure that the most effective and efficient therapy is offered for a given person and their problems. Keeping abreast of recent research through continuing professional development requires not only a reasonable memory and degree of intelligence but also a considerable degree of perseverance if you are to offer a good enough service to prospective clients.

Such perseverance is closely linked to stamina. Stamina is an attribute which will be useful not only for the rigours of training but also to enable you, as a counsellor, to remain with a person through sometimes very difficult and upsetting aspects of their life and in some cases to death, without severely affecting your ability to continue working creatively with other individuals on your counselling caseload. Supervision will play a key part in aiding this process but will alone be insufficient without a degree of stamina.

Related to stamina is the ability to focus and to see the wider picture for a client even though he or she may wander. A degree of disintegration comes with a number of difficult psychological conditions and it is essential that the counsellor is able to remain focused in the midst of such life. This focus will be better maintained if the counsellor has the ability to heighten or decrease the emotional intensity within the session.

Maturity

Whatever form of counselling, counselling psychology or psychotherapy you eventually engage in, and regardless of both the specific problem area (for example, HIV, alcohol abuse, bereavement, cancer, disfigurement, eating disorders, relationship problems, sexual abuse, sexual problems or substance misuse) and the therapeutic model which underpins your practice (for example, cognitive behavioural, multimodal, person-centred or psychodynamic), you will probably be faced with clients who are each very different from the other. Personality characteristics, socio-economic class, intelligence, education, cultural background, ethnic group, financial status, geographical location, religious and political beliefs, spiritual leanings and gender are but a few of the factors which help to make each of us unique individuals. A reasonable degree of maturity is therefore necessary to be able to interact effectively with differing individuals who present with a wide variety of problems. Part of that maturity is the ability first to realise that individuals exist within much wider systems and second to accept that you will not necessarily be able fully to understand the totality of that wider system. A recognition of this diversity coupled with appropriate training will hopefully enable you to answer the important question posed by Paul (1967): 'What treatment, by whom, is most effective for this individual with that specific problem and under which set of circumstances?'

Being a good listener

The ability to listen is an important quality in a both caring and non-caring professions, but is perhaps the most essential quality necessary for counselling. Listening has a particular meaning within counselling and if you decide to take up counselling training, some of this will be devoted to developing a range of different listening skills. But prior to training the potential counsellor will probably have the ability to listen to what other people have to say, and be able to maintain this ability in the face of individuals who may recount events which at times may not be exceptional, entertaining or interesting. If you find it difficult to listen to another person for more than a couple of sentences without jumping in with ideas and long utterances of your own, if you monopolise conversations and keep interrupting, or if you cannot curb your tendency to complete other people's sentences for them, then you may find counselling training particularly difficult.

We previously suggested that the ability to act autonomously was an important counsellor characteristic. When coupled with listening, a further quality emerges of being able to stand back or engage more fully. As you gain ever greater knowledge about psychological problems through study, it is easy to fall into the trap of believing you are ever the expert. It is important to be able to suspend your 'expert role' within sessions and demonstrate your active listening skills.

Flexibility and unconditional positive regard

Coupled with seeing others within the context of a wider system are the qualities of flexibility and open-mindedness. For example, if you are a socialist (or conservative, or Christian) and only able to value people with similar views to your own, or if you narrowly demand or deny political correctness, it will prove difficult for you to be a useful practitioner not only to those who have differing views to yours but even to those with similar views. The reason for this is that the inability to accept other people as they are, with warts and all and regardless of their views, suggests that you have rigidly held beliefs. At some level you are demanding that people be different to the way they are. This will usually be counter-therapeutic. Challenging rigidly held beliefs and helping people to adopt a philosophy of self-acceptance and acceptance of others is central to Rational Emotive Behaviour Therapy developed by Ellis (see, for example, Ellis, 1979). Recognising all humans as worthwhile in this way and being able to convey unconditional positive regard to people with different views on life to your own is a central quality in counselling. If you entirely lack this, it is likely to render you unsuitable to practise as a counsellor, counselling psychologist or psychotherapist. Rather than opening your mind and heart to others, you will be closed and judgemental. Of course, we all differ in the degree to which we are able to accept others and regard them positively. However, the quality of open-mindedness to the extent that you can positively regard others who have different views to your own goes hand in hand with being flexible. Another way in which you will benefit from the quality of flexibility is connected with the way you relate to others. If you are to relate to a wide range of people with differing views and backgrounds, the ability to adopt different styles of interaction with a client to discover the interpersonal approach that may best benefit the particular therapeutic relationship may be helpful.

The term, 'authentic chameleon' has been coined by Lazarus (1993). It is important to distinguish between being genuine and being an authentic chameleon. An analogy may help. You will probably relate to your partner, young son or daughter, older son or daughter, mother and father quite differently while being sincere with each. If one son is bright while another has learning difficulties, you will probably engage differently with each while loving both. To try to interact in the same way with each would be to deny both their individuality. Doing so would indicate a naive view of personal relationships and ignore that as a human being you may take on a wide variety of roles while retaining your authenticity or 'you-ness'. You may be just as authentic as a mother, partner, writer, musician or artist, but fulfil each of your human roles differently. Similarly, you will relate best to a wide range of individuals as a counsellor, psychotherapist or counselling psychologist if you are able to bring a range of personal styles of interaction to the counselling relationship or be an authentic chameleon.

BASIC COUNSELLING SKILLS

Within social sciences generally, a debate continues about the relative importance of nature and nurture to organisms in general and to human beings in particular. In the context of this chapter, you may ask yourself the following question: Is it possible to acquire the qualities necessary to become a counsellor? In other words, are they innate qualities or learnable skills? We believe it is a bit of both. If you had all of the qualities and skills we discuss, developed to a high degree, you would certainly have the potential to become a competent and resourceful counsellor. Few potential counsellors are fortunate enough to start from such an advanced level. To succeed as a counsellor, counselling psychologist or psychotherapist you will need to have a reasonable mix of the qualities we identify as a foundation for development. If you have none of them, it is unlikely you would succeed in such professions (but also unlikely that you would wish to be engaged in this work).

Truax and Carkhuff (1967) identify five core elements thought to be essential for good counselling to take place:

1 Be accurately empathic.
2 Be 'with' the client.
3 Be understanding, or grasp the client's meaning.
4 Communicate empathic understanding.
5 Communicate unconditional positive regard.

They later identified empathy, genuineness and warmth to be the core conditions necessary for effective counselling to take place.

Empathy

Empathy is often considered to be one of the most important qualities required by a counsellor (e.g. Rogers, 1957). Empathy is where the counsellor understands the client in a meaningful and accurate way and it can be achieved on different levels. Empathy has been likened to climbing inside the skin of another individual and taking a walk around. Some people distinguish empathy from sympathy. Sympathy has taken on a negative connotation in recent times as it has become associated with being patronising. A phrase which captures and caricatures sympathy is: 'there, there; never mind; it will all turn out okay'. Sympathy is peripheral while empathy is central and involves the whole individual in a meaningful and realistic way.

We now consider two main levels of empathy. First, the counsellor communicates his or her understanding by showing the client that he or she understands the client's world and viewpoint through both verbal and non-verbal communication. This demonstrates that the counsellor has listened and understands how the client feels. Second, the counsellor influences the client and enables him or her to dig deeper into his or her personal issues to take a more objective look at what is happening in his or her life. You will find this process requires the qualities of genuineness and respect and an ability to build rapport and gently challenge the client's perception where appropriate. Hence, advanced empathy is not simply about agreeing with a client. If you are unable to challenge or confront a client about appropriate issues, it may be that you have an overly strong need to be liked or approved of by others. This may be an obstacle to you becoming a counsellor and will require you to work on this area before moving forward (see 'Contraindications').

Genuineness can be explained as knowing yourself and like other qualities is one we all have to varying degrees. We all have many roles in life; for example, husband, wife, partner, brother, sister, parent, friend or colleague. As a counsellor it is beneficial to identify as many of your prejudices and stereotypes which contribute to your unique personality. Genuineness is being yourself in every situation and not attempting to be like another individual: you do not change your attitudes towards people just because you are in another role. This is not to be confused with the desirability for you to alter your style of interaction with different people (as described above under 'Flexibility and unconditional positive regard'). Doing so will involve you in becoming more self-aware and recognising your own feelings if you are to be viewed as an authentic person. This process requires both genuineness and flexibility.

Warmth and unconditional positive regard go hand in hand and are important factors in building a therapeutic alliance with your client provided they are successfully conveyed. Qualities of warmth are conveyed through smiling, gestures such as nods and head position and open postures. Warmth is expressed mainly through body language and non-verbal communication and is usually involuntary but can be focused upon and altered through counselling training. It is important not to force these attributes or lose them in the intensity of the moment, but to allow yourself to relax and be natural. Counsellor warmth should aid the therapeutic process and encourage your client to continue in a sometimes difficult dialogue. Counsellors disagree about the extent to which counsellor warmth be shown and some believe that minimal warmth is preferable to avoid the client developing or extending a need for approval from the therapist. However, with self-awareness on the part of the counsellor, the transmission of counsellor warmth may highlight the client's need for approval and other dependency issues which can then be explored. We believe that counsellor warmth emanates from the counsellor's genuine respect and unconditional positive regard for the client. Potential counsellors who gush warmth may be masking their own need for approval and this is something which training and the counsellor's own therapy will hopefully highlight.

Humour

Some of the traditional schools of counselling, psychotherapy and counselling psychology would view humour as a form of defence mechanism, and undoubtedly some clients cover up their emotional pain by the excessive use of humour. A number of therapists regard humour as a legitimate component of the therapuetic relationship (e.g. see Ellis, 1977) and we regard it to be important for several reasons. Before considering these, it is important for you to recognise that it is only appropriate if it is associated with one of the primary qualities we outlined above: respect for the client. If you respect the people you counsel, then any humour you may bring to a counselling situation will be born of this respect. Being so, your humour will be able to be described by others as 'laughing with' rather than 'laughing at' the client. In many counselling situations, you may find that even though your humour is congruent with respect for your client and is therefore the 'laughing with' variety, your client may think that you are 'laughing at' him or her. This is easy to appreciate as clients come into counselling with a range of sensitivities and insecurities. If a client thinks that you are laughing at (rather than with) him or her, the therapeutic relationship will probably be damaged. This is also unethical as it could be construed as harmful. In most cases, provided a good therapeutic relationship has been developed with the client, it will not be the end of the world as it may highlight or exemplify personal material the client has which may need to be worked on in therapy. Nevertheless, the use of humour in therapy is best used sparingly when you are new to counselling and its effective use as a therapeutic tool will develop as your counselling practice matures.

We now consider why therapist humour is important, but before doing so need to make a distinction between recognising humour in situations and expressing it. As discussed elsewhere in this chapter, the quality of being a good listener is fundamental to counselling. As you listen to the story of your client's life (or that part of your client's life for which counselling is sought) a very wide range of thoughts and reflections will pass through your mind and only a small proportion of these will involve humour. Of all the different thoughts, you will only express a few: those which have a therapeutic aim. Your use of humour in the counselling room is no different. It is deployed solely for therapeutic reasons which will become clearer as your training proceeds.

Therapist humour is an important quality for the therapist's own well-being as it can help in achieving a sense of balance when faced with a caseload of people's difficulties. This recognition of the humourous is usually tied in with accepting things which cannot be changed, changing things which can best be changed and recognising the difference between the two. The expression of humour within counselling is usually with these three components in mind and humour can be an important catalyst in helping clients to see things in a different and more helpful light.

PERSONAL CONTRAINDICATIONS

We will now consider some qualities or characteristics which may be detrimental to the counselling process. We noted previously that you do not need to have all of the positive qualities or characteristics we identified developed to a high degree but benefit by having a reasonable mix of them. Similarly, having some of these negative characteristics developed to a lesser degree will not necessarily prevent you from progressing to become a counsellor provided you can recognise their potential effect on the counselling process and work on these characteristics in your own therapy.

Mission to solve other people's problems

If one of your personal qualities is that you tend to want to solve other people's problems for them, this may interfere with the professional counselling process. Obviously, anyone interested in the caring professions will have a desire to help solve other people's problems, but this is very different from solving them yourself. Counselling is partly about helping others to find ways to deal effectively with their own problems by empowering or validating them to do so. In some situations this may involve you in training or coaching the client (depending on the therapeutic orientation of the counselling model you adopt), but always the client takes action – not you. To do so would take power away from the client which would be counter-therapeutic. We noted above that an effective counsellor will endeavour to understand a client's situation from their perspective by 'being in their boots'. The person with a mission to solve other people's problems tends to view those problems from their own, not the client's, point of view.

Rigidly held beliefs

We have already discussed some of the negative effects for the counselling process of you holding certain beliefs rigidly. The counselling process requires you to be flexible in your thinking and beliefs if only to understand the client. Rigidly held beliefs are often at the centre of a person's emotional or psychological distress. Some models of psychotherapy, such as Rational Emotive Behaviour Therapy (Ellis, 1994) regard rigidly held beliefs as central to emotional disturbance. Most of us have some rigidity in our beliefs, but if you hold a wide constellation of strongly held beliefs, this may prove to be counter-therapeutic.

Lack of willingness to learn and closure to feedback and inputs from others

We noted above that counselling involves a fairly well developed understanding of the client as part of a wider system (his environment) and also that as a counsellor you can be most effective by continually developing your self-awareness. Neither of these is possible if you operate as a 'closed system' and if you try to prevent others from influencing you. Some of you may find that the process of becoming more self-aware can be quite personally painful, if ultimately rewarding. This may be particularly so when large areas of awareness about yourself open up fairly quickly, such as at the beginning of counsellor training. Of course, this part of the process of counsellor training is no different from the process which your clients will undergo. If you are unwilling to learn from others, then you are unlikely to develop your self-awareness very far which will make it difficult for you to proceed as a counsellor. Another important aspect of counselling is about learning from your clients and many counsellors will attest to the fact that it is the clients or users who reveal to the counsellor some of the most important learning points which make it possible for the counsellor to develop a wealth and depth of experience about the counselling process. Similarly, if you are unwilling to listen to your supervisor (assuming that he or she is adequately trained to fulfil the supervisory role), you will find it difficult to progress very far in the field of counselling, psychotherapy or counselling psychology.

Need for approval

Few of us would deny that we enjoy or value others approving of us. This is both natural and human. But if you need all of your actions to be approved of by others and focus excessively on whether or not this or that deed would be seen as acceptable to certain others (but what about. . .) then it may be that you have turned a natural desire for approval into an absolutistic demand. As a major aspect of counselling is about change in people seeking it, a counsellor's excessive demand for approval will be counter-therapeutic. It will block you from confronting clients at appropriate points in therapy. Additionally, some clients may come across as manipulative, and some of these people will be skilled at focusing in on your need for approval, which in order to be given will lead the therapy to become stuck and unhelpful.

Major psychological illness

The codes of practice of the various organisations responsible for accrediting counsellors, psychotherapists and counselling psychologists all have a practice point which requires you to carry out your work only when you are in a fit state to do so, and to cease work (temporarily if necessary) when you are unfit. People with major psychological problems will probably find it difficult to counsel while they are in the midst of an episode of that illness as it will disrupt their ability to counsel and will also be a drain on their own system which will be struggling at such periods. Apart from this, and provided that a reasonable mix of the qualities discussed above are in place, we believe that users of psychiatric services may have an advantage over those who have not suffered as their practice will be user-led and their empathy founded upon appropriate experience.

We hope this chapter has helped you to decide whether or not you have a reasonable mix of the qualities necessary to become a competant counsellor. If you think that you lack some of the necessary qualities, it may be helpful to recognise that they may be developed to a considerable degree. This may be aided by taking an elementary counselling course, reading some introductory counselling literature, engaging in some voluntary work that involves you meeting people and dealing with their problems, considering personal therapy for yourself or engaging in a personal development programme which will include self-reflection and may include some or all of the above.

REFERENCES

Ellis, A. (1977). Fun as psychotherapy. *Rational Living*, 12(1), 2–6.

Ellis, A. (1979). The practice of rational-emotive therapy. In A. Ellis & J.M. Whitely (Eds), *Theoretical and empirical foundations of rational-emotive therapy*. Monterey, CA: Brooks/Cole.

Ellis, A. (1994). *Reason and emotion in psychotherapy* (2nd ed.). New York: Birch Lane Press.

Hanshew, E.R (1998). An investigation of the wounded healer phenomenon: counselor trainees and their self-conscious emotions and mental health. *Dissertation Abstracts International Section A: Humanities and Social Sciences*, 58(10A), 3846.

Lazarus, A.A. (1993). Tailoring the therapeutic relationship or being an authentic chameleon. *Psychotherapy, 30*, 404–407.

Paul, G.L. (1967). Strategy of outcome research in psychotherapy. *Journal of Consulting Psychology, 331*, 109–118.

Rogers, C.R. (1957). The necessary and sufficient conditions of therapeutic personality change. *Journal of Consulting Psychology, 21*(2), 95–104.

Scragg, P., Bor, R., & Watts, M. (1999). The influence of personality and theoretical models on applicants to a counselling psychology course: a preliminary study. *Counselling Psychology Quarterly, 12*(3), 263–270.

Truax, C.B., & Carkhuff, R.R. (1967). *Towards effective counselling and psychotherapy: training and practice.* Chicago: Aldine.

Watzlawick, P., Weakland, J., & Fisch, R. (1974). *Change: principles of problem formation and problem resolution.* New York: W.W. Norton.

Williams, S.C. (1999). Counselor trainee effectiveness: an examinatin of the relationship between personality characteristics, family of origin functioning, and trainee effectiveness. *Dissertation Abstracts International: Section B: The Sciences and Engineering, 59*(8-B), 4494.

7

Preparing your Application

Charles Legg

Selection for anything, be it a course, a job or membership of a sporting team, is a harrowing process and it is easy to lose sight of the fact that getting yourself selected is usually the start of your problems, not the end. It is tempting to look for ways of massaging people's impressions of you to ensure that they look on you favourably at selection, but unless you can deliver the goods afterwards, you gain little from it. Not only that, you might even find yourself in legal difficulties if it could be showed that you knowingly gave incorrect information.

This chapter is aimed at people who want to communicate accurately in their applications, not at those who wish to mislead. Since the first rule for filling in application forms is that you should tell the truth, and as the truth may debar you from certain courses, there is no magic formula for filling them in to ensure that you get offered a place. Indeed, those of us involved in selection go out of our way to ensure that there is no formula and if we find that people are providing stock answers to questions, we rapidly change our procedures. While reading this chapter will not guarantee you success in your applications, it will help to ensure that if you are unsuccessful it is not because you have answered questions in such a way as to create an unnecessarily unfavourable impression of you as a candidate. I start by discussing the purpose of our application forms and then look at the specific questions common to many of them.

WHY DO WE HAVE APPLICATION FORMS?

Application forms are complex because they try to do a number of jobs at once. We cannot offer you a place unless we know that you are interested in taking our course, so the first job of the application is to alert us to your interest. Interviewing people is a time-consuming and expensive business for all parties involved, so there is little point in calling people for interview unless we are reasonably certain that you have the characteristics we are looking for in people who successfully complete the course. Much of the information requested is aimed at assessing whether it would be in your interests to call you for interview. Student selection is carried out within the complex legal framework of equal opportunities legislation and admissions officers are aware of the fact that they may be called upon to justify their decisions before a court. They therefore have to ensure that they elicit from candidates all of the information a court might think relevant to their decision. They may also find it necessary to gather information to demonstrate that their decision making is not biased. Finally, like all businesses, training institutions want to gather information which will assist them in marketing, so they will solicit information that can be used to target marketing information more accurately. Another important reason why applications forms are complex is that they are designed to filter out casual applications and to ensure that if we receive an appropriately completed set of forms from someone they are strongly motivated to do our course.

Showing that you are interested in a course

You might think that you have already registered your interest by asking for an application form, but that only shows that you are interested in doing a course; it says nothing about your interest in doing the particular course for which you are applying. Asking for an application form is like asking for holiday brochures from a travel agent; you have shown that you are interested in going on holiday, but your destination is still unclear. Courses in psychotherapy and counselling in the UK differ from each other in a number of ways, ranging from their preferred theoretical orientations to their teaching methods and what each admissions officer wants to know is that you are aware of those differences and actually want to do the particular course they have on offer.

The only way to achieve this is to make sure that you have read all of the relevant information on the course before filling in the application form. Most courses tell you what their preferred theoretical orientations are and how strongly they are committed to the notion of having an orientation. If the prospectus announces that the centre views itself as the premier department for teaching cognitive behaviour therapy and you announce in your application that you have an abiding interest in psychodynamic approaches, or believe that people should practise eclectically, then rejection is very likely. Similarly, if the prospectus tells you that much of the teaching will take the form of large group lectures, expressing a preference for one-to-one tutorials will be met with rejection.

This means that you have to do a considerable amount of preparation before filling in application forms and possess a certain amount of honesty about your own limits. If the department to which you are applying indicates a preference for cognitive behavioural work, then you are more likely be selected if you can demonstrate a similar interest based on an understanding of what is involved. In other words, you have to go beyond saying 'I am interested in cognitive behavioural work' to saying why you are interested in terms that convince the reader of the form that you understand what it involves. The temptation is to apply all over the place, telling each admissions officer that you have a burning interest in the approach offered by their course. The danger, as I have already indicated, is that they believe you and you find yourself investing three years and several thousand pounds in studying a mode of therapy that you find personally unacceptable.

Showing that you have the competencies

There is no point in wasting your time calling you for interview if we can ascertain beforehand that you do not have the qualifications and experience we have found necessary in successful candidates on our courses. Most courses have some academic component, involving activities like essay writing and producing case studies in which your practice will be justified by reference to published therapy models, and independent research. We are, therefore interested in your prior academic achievements to be sure that you have the skills necessary to complete these course requirements.

Masters level degrees usually require you to have a bachelor's degree but vary in their insistence that you have previously studied a particular subject. Courses accredited by the British Association for Counselling and Psychotherapy (BACP) or the United Kingdom Council for Psychotherapy (UKCP) tend not to stipulate the content of prior studies. Although some courses may not stipulate the content of prior studies, they may approach psychotherapy from a philosophical or literary perspective and require evidence that you can think, research and write in an appropriate manner. If you are applying for a course recognised by the British Psychological Society (BPS) as leading to qualification as a chartered psychologist, then you simply have to have a degree in psychology that is recognised by the BPS for graduate basis of registration (GBR). If you start a course without GBR, you may find that you have to complete the requirements of the BPS before you can graduate from the course.

It is important to give as much information as you can, partly to put your achievements into context and partly to avoid the impression that you have something to hide. Five GCSEs obtained from an inner-city comprehensive have a completely different meaning from the same number obtained from one of our more expensive public schools. Obtaining a very good bachelor's degree is much more impressive in someone with a poor school record, being indicative of a specific flair or passion for a topic, than in someone who has consistently obtained high marks. If you didn't do well, don't try to hide it, because suspicious admissions officers may assume the worst. If, for example, you do not give the class of a bachelor's degree, we will tend to assume that you didn't get a first or upper second. Remember, above all, that we are trying to match your attainments to the requirements of our course, so profile of attainment may be more important than absolute level. Someone who sailed through school, trailing clouds of academic glory, before a brilliant university career may actually make a dreadful psychotherapist, because they are out of touch with everyone else, only know about the world through books and have never experienced the humbling trauma of failure. Someone who did poorly at school because they were out having a good time with their wide circle of friends, went to work at 16, and then came back to study at 30 because they had a specific reason to get a degree may be a much better candidate.

Courses also have practical elements, such as role plays and placements. Some expect you to have already had some experience on which the course will build, while others may take complete novices and guide them from scratch. Whatever our requirements, we need to know how much experience you have already had so that we can determine whether you are likely to benefit from the course we have to offer. It is vital that you give accurate information about your prior experience to ensure that you end up on a suitable course and do not find yourself in placements in which you are a danger to yourself and other people. It is also important that you convince us that you understand what you are getting into when you become a psychotherapist. Much of our work involves people who have highly destructive ways of interacting with others. Some are violent, some permanently under the influence of drugs and some so helpless and dependent that your fundamental human sympathy demands that you support and protect them. Working with such people can vary from the frustrating to the completely undermining. Before we admit people to courses we need to be sure that they understand the demands that will actually be placed on them in practice.

Giving information necessary for 'reasonable' decisions

There is a story about a British medical school that tried to automate its admissions procedure by using a complex statistical procedure to identify the characteristics of candidates who did well on its course. The procedure had to be abandoned when it was discovered that the system was simply selecting white, middle-class males who had been to particular schools because, in the past, these had been the people who had done well; not surprising in a system dominated by white, middle-class males who had gone to public schools. Although this admissions policy was highly effective in filling places with candidates who succeeded, it was deemed both racist and sexist and outlawed as a consequence.

When engaged in selection there is a powerful temptation to choose people who are like you and there is no reason to presuppose that the admissions officers of psychotherapy courses are any less prone to this sort of bias than others, although their biases may favour different groups. To prevent these biases, we need to collect information that would be deemed relevant to our decisions and information through which we can show that our decision making is unbiased. If we are going to reject you, and we have to reject some candidates simply to prevent courses becoming overloaded, we have to do so on the basis of objective criteria; it is not acceptable for us to appeal to 'gut reactions'. If we call for interview everyone who has six months experience of working in a psychotherapy setting and who obtained at least a lower second class honours degree, then we need even more information to justify rejecting someone. This may mean asking for a lot of detail about prior experience, so that we can distinguish between candidates who have acted as clerks in psychiatric hospitals and those who have spent time working directly with clients.

We also have to be able to demonstrate that we are not biased in our selection, which means gathering personal information that, paradoxically, we have to exclude from decision making. For example, we may want to know your gender, race or marital status, not because we want to base our decisions on this information but because we want to be able to show that we are not doing so. If 50 per cent of our applicants are males, but we only take in 5 per cent of male students, then we need to know that. It may be that on objective criteria which would stand up to external scrutiny it was appropriate to reject such a large proportion of male candidates, but the onus is on us to monitor the situation and ensure that this is the case.

Gathering marketing information

Like it or not, psychotherapy courses have to pay for themselves. We have to raise sufficient income from fees, grants and endowments to be able to cover the full costs of providing our courses, or else we get closed down. Since fees make up a huge proportion of our incomes, it is vital that we maintain a steady stream of suitably qualified applicants who will pay fees in subsequent years. Sometimes courses manage this by word-of-mouth recommendations, but most of us find that we also have to advertise. The problem is to work out the target audience for our advertising and the best sort of 'sales pitch' for that audience. This often means trying to build up a profile of successful applicants, by asking for information about the newspapers and magazines they read, family income and age, so that we target our limited resources effectively.

Deterring applicants

Being involved in admissions is hard work. You have to read large numbers of application forms and then arrange interviews for lots of candidates. If, at the end of it all, applicants don't turn up for interview or don't accept places that they have been offered, then you have not been working very efficiently. Under the circumstances, it is inevitable that admissions procedures have become more complex, so as to filter out those who are not motivated to do the course. One of the best ways of assessing someone's motivation for something is to determine the obstacles they are prepared to overcome to get it. If you will only buy an ice-cream if you happen to stumble across a vendor in the course of your travels, then your motivation for eating it is probably low. If you are prepared to walk all over a strange town in search of one, you probably have a strong motivation to eat ice-cream. We tend to approach our courses in the same way. If someone can get an interview by just phoning up and expressing interest, then people with low motivation to do the course will apply. If there is a 30-page application form, then only those who are strongly motivated to do the course are likely to spend the time filling it in. A further benefit to us is that the more effort you have had to put into completing the application form, the more you are likely to value the course if you are invited for interview or offered a place.

COMMON QUESTIONS YOU SHOULD BE PREPARED TO ANSWER

Personal details

Most application forms ask for a considerable amount of personal detail, much of which will appear irrelevant to deciding whether to offer you a place, and the temptation is to skip these questions. That is unhelpful because much of this information is necessary for us to determine whether we are complying with equal opportunities legislation while the rest usually has to do with immigration law. We cannot use information about your race or gender to decide whether to admit you, so you need have no fear about giving that information. We desperately need this information to ensure that we are not inadvertently discriminating against people. Information about disability is also particularly important because failure to communicate about a problem may mean that you cannot subsequently make a claim against an institution for failing to meet your needs.

Most institutions charge significantly higher fees to 'overseas' students than to 'home' candidates, so it is tempting for those applying from outside the UK or the EU to pretend that they are 'home' students. Apart from the fact that this constitutes fraud and could leave you liable to criminal proceedings, this may also run foul of immigration law. British law is very precise about those who are allowed to reside and, more particularly, work in the UK, favouring exclusion over inclusion, but we make exceptions in the case of genuine students. However, you should be aware that prior study in the UK or EU does not count towards a qualifying period of residence for the purpose of being considered a home student. If you are an overseas applicant, the institution to which you are applying will assist you with the immigration authorities, providing they know that you are an 'overseas' student. The immigration authorities take a very dim view of people who claim to be students for the purpose of residing in the UK but then claim UK or EU residence for other purposes.

Some institutions also want to know about your finances. Education is a labour intensive service for which colleges and universities receive relatively little subsidy, so most full-time courses cost as much as a second-hand car (£4000–£5000 pa at 2001 prices). The difference between cars and courses is that the former can always be repossessed if you default on payments, but it is difficult to claim back an education; hence we are keen on ensuring that you can pay before offering you a place. Even if there is not an explicit question about how you are going to pay your fees on the form, you should certainly have given this issue some thought and be prepared to discuss it at interview.

Qualifications

Most institutions want to know a lot about your education, some going back to A-levels or equivalents and possibly asking about GCSEs or O-levels. Some people, particularly mature applicants, cannot remember all the details of their schooling. If that is the case, estimate the number but make it clear that you have done so. Even if you cannot remember all the details, it does help if you can remember whether you obtained qualifications in English and mathematics, since many courses require a minimum level of competence in these.

We are particularly interested in your university studies and professional qualifications, because these represent your most recent attainments and involve subjects most relevant to your interest in psychotherapy and counselling. Some application forms can be quite intimidating, because they leave a huge amount of space in which to detail these qualifications, and 'BSc Hons, Philosophy' tends to look a bit lost in the space. Don't worry about this. It usually happens because institutions use the same application form for a whole range of postgraduate courses. For example, at my own institution, City University, a counselling psychology student can do up to four separate courses before finishing the entire programme, starting with a postgraduate certificate and finishing with a D.Psych. By the time they are applying for the D.Psych, most of our candidates have a lot to write in the relevant space.

Admissions staff tend to be very experienced at reading between the lines of application forms, so there is not a lot of point in fudging the issue where you think that your qualifications are inadequate. Nearly all universities in the UK divide second-class degrees into upper and lower seconds. If you state that you received a second class-degree, it will be assumed that it was a lower second and that you are embarrassed by the fact. Given the importance of genuineness in therapeutic relationships, your embarrassment may count against you more than your actual degree class, since it indicates that you are not comfortable with who you are and seek to create false impressions.

If you are applying as an overseas applicant, give your qualifications in the way that is recognised in your own country. Do not attempt to offer UK equivalents by saying that you have A-levels when, in fact, you passed the Baccalaureate. Most institutions have staff who are expert in advising on the standing of qualifications and we would prefer to ask their advice rather than put the onus on candidates to decide on equivalencies. The situation is particularly complex if you applying for a course recognised by the British Psychological Society as a basis for becoming a 'chartered' psychologist, because they have to give separate approval for overseas qualifications. It may turn out that your degree is acceptable to a training institution but not the BPS. For this reason, you should take questions about whether your degree gives your graduate basis of registration very seriously. Those applying as overseas students with non-UK degrees should check their status with the BPS before applying.

Most institutions expect overseas applicants whose first language is not English to demonstrate competence in English through a recognised qualification. These qualifications are best viewed as necessary but not sufficient for surviving on a psychotherapy or counselling course. You will not get on the course without one, but you should be under no illusion about having a sufficient command of English to function effectively as a therapist, unless you have much more experience of talking, writing and reading in English. This means that you should be prepared to document whatever else you have done to improve your English.

Work experience

The primary purpose of this section is for you to be able to indicate the experience you have had that justifies your belief that you should train as a psychotherapist or counsellor. For this reason, most application forms include part-time and voluntary work, as well as full-time paid employment. No one expects candidates to have devoted their entire lives to psychotherapy since leaving school, but we do expect to see some evidence of relevant work. If you have only ever been an investment banker, your decision to become a therapist may not be taken very seriously. If you have been an investment banker who spent her evenings as a Samaritans volunteer, the decision becomes much more plausible. The other purpose of this section is to get a sense of you as a person, particularly the way that you have used your opportunities. It may not be used at the initial selection stage, but may be the basis of quite searching questions at interview.

Experience of psychotherapy and counselling

Many application forms explicitly ask you for details of your experience of working as a therapist. If they ask about this, it is functioning as a filtering question and you are unlikely to get on the course unless you can say something positive. Since these courses tend to have demanding placements, in which you will be expected to apply your skills fairly soon after joining the course, it is unwise to massage the details because you can rapidly find yourself out of your depth. Not only is this unethical, but being in a therapeutic relationship with which you cannot cope can damage you as well. If you have any doubts about the level of prior experience required, check with the course managers before filling in the form.

Some application forms also ask you whether you have had experience as a client. This may seem unnecessarily intrusive, but the only reason for asking is to give you another opportunity to talk about your experiences of therapy when you come to interview. We will not dwell on the issues that took you to therapy but will focus, instead, on your understanding of the therapeutic process and the insights you gained about the needs of clients and the techniques of therapists.

Personal statement/further information

Most applicants find this the most daunting section, because it asks for an essay rather than recitation of facts. The goal of this section is for you to convince the admissions team that you are a serious candidate for the course for which you are applying, using the word 'serious' in its two meanings. First and foremost, you must show that your experience fits you for the course, so that you can be given serious attention as an applicant, but you must also show that you are motivated to do the course and that you take the application seriously. Writing a personal statement is a little like preparing a television advertisement because you have a very small space to get across the merits of your product – you – and create the best possible impression.

It may help if you break up this section into a series of issues and write a little piece that addresses each of them. Of these, the most important is why you want to work as a psychotherapist or counsellor and we are looking for positive reasons, based on prior experience. Statements like 'I did a lot a voluntary work at university and, on graduating, I trained with the Samaritans. I have found this work rewarding, and my supervisors tell me that I have a flair for the work, but I am frustrated by my lack of detailed knowledge.' are the sort for which we are looking. Statements like 'I am fed up with my present job and fancy a change' do not impress. We expect you to have a sense of where the qualification will lead you, which means being realistic while basing your ambitions on evidence that suggests that they are likely to be fulfilled. If, for example, you fancy setting up a private practice, we would expect you to tell us about your discussions with GPs who could refer to you and how you would obtain and pay for consulting rooms.

Telling us about what you expect to get out of our particular course would also help. Statements like 'I am particularly drawn to the course at [insert name of institution] because [insert reason]' are a good idea. A little sycophancy often helps at this point, particularly if you can explain how your interest in the subject was kindled or fostered by a book written by one of the teaching staff. This part of the statement tells us that you have read our course material properly and understand what you are getting into. If you cannot think of any convincing reason why you do want to do a particular course, you should probably tear up the application form at this point.

The other main use of this section is to try to explain away gaps in your employment history or qualifications. If you didn't work for three years, this is the bit of the form where you explain why. These days, many people have career breaks for activities like travelling or having children while others will have been unemployed because of difficulties in the job market. These will not be held against you if you explain them, but if you don't people might assume the worst. Most admissions regulations have the word 'normally' liberally distributed through them to allow institutions to admit individuals who do not have conventional qualifications. The personal statement is the point at which you convince the admissions staff that you fall into this category, if it is appropriate. The onus is on you to explain why your other experience should be counted as the equivalent of, for example, doing a degree. Perhaps you trained for the clergy in your particular faith, taking a qualification respected within your religion but not considered by itself to be the equivalent of a degree. Perhaps you were an officer in the armed forces, having attended officer training programmes rather than doing a degree. Even if you have experience that is equivalent to a degree, there will still be the matter of GBR for many courses and, like overseas candidates, you will have to confirm the acceptability of your qualifications separately with the BPS. In most instances, they will probably ask you to take their qualifying examination.

References

Many institutions are very explicit about who they will accept as referees, while others appear more liberal. However, since the purpose of the reference is the same in all instances, you should be conservative in your choices, even when not explicitly required to do so. References usually serve two separate purposes, one being to check on your honesty, the other to gain additional information about your abilities and peculiarities. For them to serve either of these purposes, institutions need some sort of quality control on referees, to be sure that they are likely to tell the truth and that they are qualified to make the judgements which they are asserting. To be able to write authoritatively about your abilities, they also need to be someone who knows you fairly well.

In order to satisfy these requirements, references are best obtained from recognised institutions like universities, schools, hospitals and local authorities, which are likely to be there some time and from which some redress might be possible if an employee has knowingly or negligently written an inaccurate reference. Failing that, individuals in private practice can be acceptable, providing they are on recognised professional registers with bodies like the BAC, BPS or UKCP, which have ethical codes that would prevent members writing dishonest references on behalf of potential trainees. References from your best friend, a neighbour or your aunt are not warranted in this way and will generally be treated with suspicion. When applying for a postgraduate course, there should be no problem with obtaining an appropriate reference because you will have had to have had appropriate experience in a relevant institution, or working with a recognised professional, to be acceptable anyway.

Referees have to be people who know you, so that their comments can be backed up by detailed observations. The most damning reference is the one that makes it clear that the author knows nothing about you, not the one that is negative. Indeed, a negative reference at least shows that the referee has attended to you. If you are applying from an educational institution, your best referees are people like your personal tutor or your dissertation supervisor. If you are applying from a job, your best referees are immediate line managers. For most courses, an ideal combination would be an academic reference and a professional one. Most admissions staff expect you to use people like this as your referees. They will be suspicious if you have not done so and may well ask for an explanation if you do not choose appropriate referees. In some instances, they may ask for additional references before making a decision.

When choosing referees, remember that they are professional people and they do not have to like you to be able to write dispassionate references, so having had a poor relationship with an appropriate referee is not a reason not to use them unless their behaviour has been clearly unacceptable in some way. Most admissions staff are aware of the complexities of working relationships, and of the power imbalances they entail, so they will usually be sympathetic if you explain why you have not chosen the obvious person as a referee. Saying 'I don't think she liked me' is not very convincing, but saying 'He told me that I wouldn't get a good reference unless I slept with him' is. Having said that, you should remember that the UK has quite draconian laws on defamation and you shouldn't say things like that about professional people unless you can substantiate them in some way.

Modern colleges and universities have such poor student–staff ratios that they make Dickens' Dotheboys Hall look like a paragon of progressive education. While you may remember your teachers (they were those harassed looking specks at the ends of hangar-sized lecture theatres), it is quite likely that they will not remember you, particularly if you are asking for a reference a year or so after graduating. Indeed, it is quite possible that they will not be there to remember you because they have retired or moved to more lucrative employment. It is always therefore sensible to write to the people you wish to use as referees before you make your applications, asking them if they would mind you using their name and bringing them up to date with your career since graduating. This is usually best done by letting them have a copy of your current CV.

Overseas candidates should make their referees aware that educational references in the UK are expected to be balanced appraisals of candidates, rather than recommendations. We expect your referees to say negative things about you and will be much more inclined to take their praise seriously if it is tempered with honest criticism. All candidates should note that we always interpret references in context, both of the other references and of the application itself. If both referees say that you are a wonderful person, then we will be inclined to believe them. If one says you are wonderful and the other hints that you are the devil incarnate, then we will conclude that you are a complex person who comes across differently to different people. If your application form says that your placement has given you experience of phenomenological psychotherapy and your referee indicates that the institution consistently works with a systemic framework, then you have a problem.

THE COVERING LETTER

It is a courtesy to write a letter that goes along with your application form to explain what the form is for and from whom it has come. This greatly assists administrators and secretaries and assures that your application to study psychotherapy does not end up in the department of phytology. At this point, you may be getting worried that your application form does not do you justice and feel the urge to put more information in the letter. Resist this urge at all costs. If you have really missed out something essential, then you should rewrite the application to include it. If you have not, then repeating yourself in your application form will only weaken your presentation.

There may be occasions on which you have to contact the institution about your application. For example, you may need to find out whether they will accept your qualifications or whether you can get exemptions from part of the course. If this is the case, you should write separately, ideally to the person who makes the relevant decisions. You can then use this information to structure your personal statement.

STYLE

Application forms require exactly the same style as all other good writing and should be models of clarity, conciseness and honesty. Most of the time, the forms are laid out to impose the first two on you, leaving you only responsible for the third, but some do not. For example, when asking for your employment history most forms indicate that they want to know the dates, the employer and the job title, but City University's form also asks you for the 'nature of duties'. This should not be treated as an invitation to give a day in the life of a psychology technician but requires simple statements like 'administering tests' and 'report writing' which highlight the distinctive features of the job. Sometimes you are obliged to deal with logical inconsistencies, like being invited to give the grades of qualifications you have yet to obtain. Be sensible and leave gaps if you do not have the information, rather than saying that you have got a 2.1 when all that has happened is that your tutor has told you that you are likely to get one.

The fact that there is space on a form does not mean that you have to fill it. However, unless it specifically invites you to continue on additional pages, it is wise to assume that you are not expected to exceed its bounds. This is particularly important with personal statements, where it is wise to prepare a draft before transferring it to the form, to ensure that it will fit in the space. There are no hard and fast rules about how much you should write, because that depends on your circumstances. A personal statement that attempts to explain why you are trying to make the transition from being a member of parliament to becoming a psychotherapist is going to be longer than one that explains why you are trying to get on a course from working in a mental health setting into which you entered immediately on graduating with a psychology degree three years ago. No matter how much you have to say, the style should always be concise, using direct statements like: 'I want to be a psychotherapist because . . .'; I believe I will make an effective psychotherapist because . . .'. It may help to use lists rather than more complex prose: 'My reasons for applying for this course are: (1) its focus on transactional analysis; (2) the international reputation of the staff; (3) the reputation of graduates of the course'. You can also be concise because you can refer across to other sections of your form. For example, you can refer to your employment history without having to repeat the details of all the relevant jobs you have held, because those details are elsewhere on the form. Indeed, when giving this supporting information, it is a good idea to avoid referring to facts that are not presented elsewhere.

Honesty means honesty with facts, not opinions. Application forms are not academic essays in which you debate the pros and cons of your being given a place on a course but exercises in marketing. You are expected to present yourself in the best possible light, compatible with the facts, rather than offer alternative interpretations of them. It is perfectly acceptable to present a 2.2 degree as evidence of your balanced life and lack of neurotic concern with academic achievement, providing you can offer independent evidence of academic competence. You can even turn your total panic when faced with statistics into a principled rejection of positivist science.

Whatever you do, try to be conservative in style because your application form is a public document. At best, it will be circulated among the staff involved in selection before they decide not to call you for interview. At worst, you will be offered a place and your application form will form the basis of a personal file that can be consulted by the people who are teaching you when they want information for things like references. If there ever were any litigation surrounding a course, your application form could even end up as an exhibit in a court case. A further reason for writing conservatively is that you will be judged on the way in which you write and one of the things for which we will be looking is your ability to match your actions to the context. To put it bluntly, if you cannot see that it is inappropriate to produce a disorganised, jokey application form, you might not be able to see that other behaviours are inappropriate when working with clients.

A final thought on style concerns physical presentation. Some organisations, my own included, produce application forms with small boxes printed on folded A3 sheets that do not fit into most computer printers. It is difficult, if not impossible, to use word processors to complete these forms and you will have to fill them in by hand. If like me you have poor handwriting, this can be something of a problem for the poor souls who have to read the application form, especially after it has been copied. One way round this is to print out things like your personal statement and glue them in to the original; another is to find someone with a printer than can take large format paper. It may also be possible to photocopy onto the original form, using the right copier. The important point is that academics, unlike merchant banks, tend not to use graphologists to assist in selecting people so we are much more concerned with being able to read your form than with having a sample of you writing.

PARTING COMMENTS

When filling in application forms remember that their primary purpose is to match your abilities and interests to the demands of the course. We do not reject people because we are intellectual or social snobs but because there are other candidates more suited to what we have to offer. Training to become a psychotherapist or counsellor is intellectually, emotionally and financially draining and places massive demands on the resources of the individuals involved. Being accepted onto a course when you do not have the necessary skills or experience can be highly damaging for all of the parties involved and the presence of unskilled or inexperienced candidates can be highly disruptive for other students. If you do not currently have the competencies that fit you to a particular course, you really do not want to be on it.

All of this means that there is only one rule for filling in application forms: *tell the truth*.

8

Preparing for an Interview

Christine Parrott

The letter arrives in the mail and momentarily you are ecstatic: you have been granted an interview for a counselling course. But the feeling is momentary. You then realize you have an interview and the anxiety begins to spread. What will the interview be like? What can you expect? What should you wear? How should you present yourself? How will you know what to say? What are the interviewers looking for? How can you make the interviewers realize that you are the person for whom they have been searching? These are all questions that this chapter aims to address.

PRACTICE MAKES PERFECT

An interview is a complex and sometimes stressful process. However, with a little preparation, you should be able to enter an interview with confidence and to present yourself well. You probably spent many hours preparing the application that secured you this interview. You now need to spend time preparing for the interview that may secure you a place on the course.

Making a good impression at an interview depends on your having practiced and done some research beforehand. Think of an interview as you would any other event for which you want to perform well: if you want to win at football, you practice; if you are in a play, you rehearse your role; if you are learning to drive a car, you repeatedly have to get behind the wheel and take to the road under supervision. Likewise, a good interview depends on preparing before you arrive, as an interview is a type of performance.

YOUR OBJECTIVES

Interviews are an artificial process. In everyday life, you hardly ever sit down in front of a group of strangers and begin talking about yourself. You do not normally enter a room and allow the majority of the conversation to be about you and your accomplishments. But you will in an interview, so the process can feel awkward if you are not prepared. What you must remember is that an interview is actually a two-way process: you and the interviewers have objectives. You want to make the best impression possible and they want to select the best people possible. An interview is not an antagonistic environment as many people often feel. It is an environment where you actually have very compatible objectives with your interviewers. Focusing on this common objective can help to make the interview a more positive experience. Think of an interview as your opportunity to present yourself at your best.

But you will need to sell yourself to the interviewers. Remember, they are looking for the best candidates to enrol in the course. Therefore, you not only have to make a good impression, but also you need to make one which is better than others. You need to make an impression that will stand out in the interviewers' minds. In order to do this, you will need to be prepared. You will need to know what you can expect in an interview, how you should present yourself, and what practical aspects will best help you achieve your goals.

TYPES OF INTERVIEWS

Interviews can take various forms and will be structured accordingly. As such, you are advised to do some detective work to find out which type of interview you can expect to encounter. Your invitation to the interview may contain information about the type of interview given. If not, however, you may want to enquire about the type of interview when you call to confirm your allotted time. Do call about your interview whether or not you plan on attending. Interview slots are limited and you have a responsibility to your fellow candidates and to the interviewers to cancel your interview if you do not wish to continue in the selection process. If you cannot make the time given, you may ask for another time but try only to do so when absolutely necessary. You do not want to become a difficult prospect before you ever attend lecture one.

Individual or group

You will either be interviewed by an individual or by a panel of interviewers, and you will either be on your own or among a group of possible candidates. For some colleges, you may even have a combination of these variations such as a panel interview followed by a group interview. Each type of interview has its benefits and drawbacks, but all can be handled to your advantage with a bit of preparation. In an individual interview, you will be the only candidate in the room. As such, the entire focus of the interview will be on you. This can produce anxiety as you will have to be 'on' at all times, but it will also allow you to have centre stage for an extended period of time. An individual interview can be to your benefit as you can answer questions fully without influence from other people and you may be able to address details in your history that would be inappropriate in a group interview.

In a group interview you are unlikely to be asked to elaborate on your experience as a volunteer at a children's play centre or on your work at the local woman's shelter. These questions are too specific for a group environment. Questions in a group interview, where as many as ten other candidates may be present, tend to be more general in nature, and you will need to personalise your answer. If in a group interview the question is presented on how one might handle an hysterical patient, you would be best not only to answer the question but to highlight any experience you may have had in this area which would help you to cope with the situation. For example, you might say:

> Well, I would give the client the space to express his feelings while remaining calm myself. I have worked on a crisis hotline for homeless people in the past and have found that sometimes the opportunity to express feelings is often of great benefit. For example, I once had a man call who was sobbing so hard I could barely understand him. But I just listened and allowed him the time to tell his story despite how difficult it was to initially understand him. In the end, he calmed down enough so that I could ask a few questions and we were able to think of some things he could do to get through the night. I think my remaining calm helped to steady him and the space he had to express his feelings seemed to help him tremendously.

Non-specific questions may also be asked in an individual setting and a similar answer would be appropriate. However, questions are generally more personal in nature in individual interviews and as such you may not always have to take the initiative yourself to enter into specifics. Remember, in both contexts, adding personal elements helps you to create a persona that will make you stand out among other candidates.

In group interviews, not only may the questions be more general in nature, but you may also be asked to role play or interact with the other candidates in the group. This is to assess how well you can think on your feet and how you interact with other individuals. In a counselling related interview, the interviewers will be looking for individuals who are comfortable interacting with others and who seem to be 'group players'. As such, it is essential that you do not openly compete with other candidates. The more relaxed and friendly you appear with others, the more favorable impression you will make. Although in essence you are competing for spaces with these individuals, you must treat them as if they were your co-workers at a job.

You need to be aware of both the content of your answers and the manner in which you deliver that content. This latter part is often referred to as the 'process' of your interview. Process issues cover that which is conveyed through body language, tone of voice, eye contact, appearance, energy level – all that is said besides the actual words. Process issues are extremely important in counselling. You will spend much time training to be aware and to respond to them in your course. As an interviewee, you will want to give the impression that you are cognizant about process issues by appropriately managing the delivery of your answers.

In addition, you may have to build upon answers given by other individuals instead of simply agreeing with their responses. In a group, someone may answer a question exactly as you would have answered it yourself. When you are given the opportunity to comment, you need not think of an entirely different answer, as you are best to be genuine with your response. However, you might try to add something personal to your reply. Remember, your goal is to stand out as a unique candidate with more potential than others. If you simply agree with someone else, the other person will be remembered for the response. If you add something of your own, you create the possibility of being remembered as well.

The panel

Another type of interview you may encounter is an interview given by a panel. In this type of environment you are likely to be on your own as a candidate but you will have several individuals asking you questions and assessing your answers. A panel interview can often be more intimidating for interviewees, but it does have some hidden advantages that can be helpful to keep in mind. For instance, a panel interview does reduce the risk of bias so that snap judgements about you are less likely to be made. In addition, a mismatch in personality with one of the interviewers is not as likely to harm your chances as in a one-on-one environment. Panel interviews also increase the number of interests present in the room. This means that you have a greater probability of covering a subject in which at least one of the interviewers has an interest. Thus, all in all, a panel interview can be advantageous for the candidate.

From a practical standpoint, panel interviews can be tough for the interviewee as there are more names to remember, more people with whom to make eye contact and a less personal atmosphere. To counteract these drawbacks, try to remain focused and conversational. Always begin to answer a question by addressing the individual who asked the question. During your answer you may make eye contact with other panel members as well, but keep the majority of your eye contact with the person who instigated the question. This will help to reduce the formality often created by the panel environment.

At the end of the interview, take care to address your questions to a particular individual. This would normally be to the 'head' inter-viewer, the person who opened the interview and appears to co-ordinate its flow, unless you have a question that is reasonably addressed to a particular panel member. For example, if you wanted to know about the online research facilities at the school and the computer librarian is on the panel, you could address him directly. This would help to show that you can discern the different roles of the panel members. However, you should only address particular panel members other than the head when you are absolutely sure that your question is appropriate to them. If you are unsure, then you are best to direct your question to the head interviewer and then allow her to guide it to the appropriate person.

ADDITIONAL PRACTICAL ISSUES

Regardless of whether your interview is individual, group or panel, you will have some practical aspects that will need to be addressed before each and every interview. These matters will help you to make a favourable impression before you ever speak a word. They include time issues, your appearance and your body language.

Time

No matter what you do in the interview, be on time for it. Your interviewers have gone through immense preparation to arrange and schedule appointment times. Your punctuality will convey your respect for their efforts and the interest you have in attending the school. If you are late, you send a message that the course is not the top priority in your life – something else has come first which has interfered with your being on time. Tardiness also gives the impression that you do not manage your time effectively – something that is crucial for counsellors in today's busy healthcare environment.

In order to ensure that you are on time, prepare your journey to the school beforehand. Determine how you will get there and how long the journey will take under adverse conditions. Do not expect your journey to go smoothly the day of your interview. Allow some time in your planning for the tube to be late, traffic on the roads, or overfilled buses. If you are unsure about the length of your journey, you might want to do a 'test run' beforehand by simply travelling to the school and locating the room where the interview will be held. Indeed, if you are unfamiliar with a school campus you will want to pinpoint the location of the interview room before the actual day you arrive. Many campuses are large and though you may arrive on time to the school, you may end up being late for your interview because you had a 20-minute walk to the appropriate building.

Prepare what you will bring and wear to the interview the night before. Have your bus or tube pass, money, keys, directions, notes, questions (addressed later), and any other items you wish to bring with you packed and ready by the door. Few things will make you more anxious on the day of your interview than to be running around your home at the last minute trying to locate your keys or the questions you spent time preparing. Moreover, decide what you are going to wear at least the day before the interview, if not earlier.

Appearance

Remember the old saying 'You never have a second chance to make a first impression'? Nowhere is this more true than in an interview situation. Your appearance will speak volumes to your interviewers the moment you step through the door. Like it or not, you will be judged on your appearance. Your interviewers have relatively very little time to access who you are so they will utilise everything at their disposal. Your clothes and personal grooming do say something about you. On a daily basis, you dress to express an image of yourself to the world and you will want to express an appropriate image to your interviewers. As such, you will need to think about the message you wish to send and which clothes in your wardrobe will help to send it.

Normally, you will want to dress 'smart casual' unless the college is a highly formal environment. In this latter case, a formal suit may be most appropriate. However, for most interviews you will not need to wear such formal attire. Trousers and a pressed shirt, a dress, or a casual day suit are suitable. A general rule is to keep things simple. Large earrings, busy shirts, or 'loud' ties can distract your interviewers. You may wear these on a daily basis to express yourself, but you are better to express your personality in words rather than with attire that detracts from the substance of what you are saying. Be smart but simple in your attire.

When picking out what you will wear, ask yourself 'what image do I want to give?' and just as importantly, 'what image does the college want to give?' The image the college is interested in creating is important to take into account. Although you may be unconventional in your dress, you need to ask yourself if this sort of image is what the college is trying to create. Ask yourself 'would the college be happy to put a picture of me at this interview on the front cover of their prospectus?' Although you may think that the college should be more accepting of different styles of dress, a first time interview is not the place to make your stand. In an interview, you do best to cater to the formality of the occasion. This does not mean that you have to be totalitarian with your style, but that you may want to be respectful of the college's image by tailoring your appearance accordingly.

Finally, before walking out the door to your interview, check your personal grooming. You will want your hair to be combed, your shoes polished, your nails clean, your clothes free of cat hair, etc. These small details are very important. You do not want your overall appearance to be tarnished by shoes that look as if they ran the London marathon. Something so out of place will surely be what the interviewer remembers instead of your carefully thought out attire. This is especially true of bad breath. Nothing is more distracting than trying to dodge someone's halitosis. As such, you might want to pop a breath mint before heading into the interview room (but make sure you have finished it before you start to speak). Chewing gum during an interview is not recommended.

Body language

Think of the following two scenarios: You are about to be introduced to your best friend's new partner. This partner walks into the room with his/her head down and shoulders slouched. When he/she goes to shake your hand, he/she fails to look you in the eye, gives you a weak handshake and mumbles something you can barely hear.

Or: You are about to be introduced to your best friend's new partner. This partner walks into the room with his/her head held high, searching cheerily for you and your friend. On finding you, he/she smiles, walks confidently over to you and extends a handshake that is firm and inviting. With a big grin, he/she then says, 'So nice to meet you!'

Which person would you rather meet? Which person would you rather have attend your college? How you carry yourself and your overall body language is as important to your interview as is anything you might say or have written in your application. In conveying a message, research has indicated that as much as 65 per cent of that message is given by your tone of voice and body language. The actual words only account for approximately 35 per cent (Straw & Shapiro, 1995). As such, you will need to ensure that you are as practiced in your body language as you are with your answers.

Overall throughout the interview, you will want to appear relaxed and interested. Try, if you can, to get plenty of sleep the night before so that you are not yawning or having trouble keeping your eyes open. When you enter the interview room you will want to:

- hold your head high;
- make eye contact with the interviewer(s);
- shake hands firmly when offered;
- walk with confidence;
- shut the door behind you.

Once seated you will want to:

- keep your head high and maintain eye contact;
- avoid fidgeting in your chair;
- keep your hands relatively still, either in your lap or on the arms of the chair;
- avoid small anxious habits such as nail biting, scratching, or foot tapping.

When speaking, you will want to:

- speak in an audible clear voice;
- vary the pitch of your voice so that it sounds energetic;
- sound convincing and confident with your replies.

Overall you are trying to convey the image of someone who is relaxed, confident and interested. As such, you will want to make sure that your body language is in keeping with this ideal. You might want to practice creating this image beforehand by sitting in front of a mirror and watching yourself as you speak. This exercise will help you to catch distracting habits and unflattering expressions of which you are not normally conscious.

DO YOUR RESEARCH

In addition to the practical tips noted above, you also need to do some research in order to prepare for your interview. This will not only help you to convey confidence, but will also demonstrate to the interviewers your interest in attending their particular school. The two areas you will want to research before attending any interview are: the school and yourself.

The college

Each school has a different philosophy and aims in its academic curriculum. Although, many colleges may appear similar, each will pride itself on the particular way in which the college approaches education. A sharp interviewee will want to learn about these differences. Your ability to speak knowledgeably about the school where you are applying will demonstrate both your interest and intelligence. Before going to the interview, telephone and get a prospectus if you do not already have one. Read it over and note the areas of research at the college as well as the principles used for learning. You can then use this information to help express your interest and to ask informed questions. For example, 'I noticed in the prospectus that you encourage field-based learning. Can you tell me what type of support the school offers in achieving this?' or 'I am particularly keen on behavioural approaches to counselling and am aware that Professor Smith has published several books on this approach. How involved will he be in the Master's level program?'

When you research a college for an interview, think to yourself 'Why them?' What makes the college of particular interest to you? What does it offer that makes it special? This is the type of information that will help you to convey your eagerness in attending the course. Interviewers are looking for a good 'match' for the college – someone who will thrive in their academic environment because of similar interests and goals. The more you express your knowledge of the college and your compatible aims, the more you will increase your appeal to the interviewers. However, beware of asking questions about which you are not genuinely interested. Such questions will sound false and detract from the favourable impression you wish to make.

When researching the particulars of a college, you will also want to refresh your memory with the specifics of the course for which you have applied. Again, like each college, each course will have unique elements that you may wish to address in your interview. You may want to think about how you fulfil the requirements of the course. In this way, you will be able to highlight areas that make you a solid candidate for the course and to address any areas in which your interviewers might see you as underqualified. In addition, knowledge of the course particulars will help you to formulate questions for your interviewers. At the appropriate point in an interview you will want to ask questions of your interviewers as it will once again demonstrate your high level of interest. Questions that demonstrate knowledge of the course also convey your enthusiasm. Questions that could have been answered by simply reading the course prospectus demonstrate your indifference.

Yourself

Just as you will need to research each college, you will also need to research yourself. Although this may sound strange, it is the most important part of your preparation process for an interview. Just as you asked the question 'Why them?' for your research on the school, here you will need to ask yourself 'Why me?' You will need to start thinking about what are your best qualities and what will make you stand out from among all the other candidates. In essence, why should the school pick you?

To answer this question, you will need to think about yourself in depth so that you can clearly articulate your strengths and weaknesses. You might want to approach your exploration as if you were selling your car. Let's say you have driven your Ford car for five years and feel that you are very familiar with it. You know it takes about 50 litres of petrol and that will last you about two weeks driving in the city. You know that it has a slight problem starting in cold weather so you often get up a few minutes early for the first morning start. It has electric windows and car seats, but the passenger seat height adjustment is not working, and the car has been driven approximately 20,000 miles. You feel you know this car pretty well.

But, in order to sell your car, you might actually be better off if you did a little investigating. For instance, you might want to calculate the actual miles per gallon that the car does so that you can use its great fuel consumption as a selling point to potential buyers. You might want to find out if the cold weather starting problem can be remedied and how much that will cost buyers to fix. Imagine how much better your car would sound if you were also knowledgeable about Ford's overall reliability and their servicing capabilities so that you could tell buyers that the car can be serviced locally and usually within 48 hours of contact. You might want to read the car owner's manual for the first time. There you could discover that the red button on the dashboard unlocks the boot from the inside, that your side view mirrors are electronically operated, and that your car is capable of being modified to increase the performance.

All these small details would help you to sell the car. Suddenly, the car with which you thought you were familiar takes on a new light and even you begin to reassess its value. Just by doing a bit of research, you have some excellent selling points to help entice buyers. This is the same principle behind researching yourself. You may be familiar with you, but with a little extra research, you will be able to articulate some finer details that will make you more enticing to interviewers. Remember you need to answer the question, 'Why me?' Lots of other people will be trying to sell themselves to the interviewers, just as lots of other people are trying to sell their car. You added value to your car by being able to speak knowledgeably about it, and you will add value to yourself by being able to do likewise.

To research yourself, you will want to sit down and spend some time thinking about what makes you special. Ask yourself the following questions and make notes to yourself on paper. This will make it easier for you to recall your thoughts and then build a solid profile of yourself:

- What are my best qualities?
- How can I contribute to this particular programme?
- What makes me fit into this particular programme?
- What qualities do I have that have contributed to my success?
- What qualities do I have that will make me a good counsellor/ therapist?
- What ten achievements make me special?
- How has my past shaped my personality?
- What extra-curricular activities add to my profile as a counsellor?
- What makes me want to be a counsellor/therapist?
- Do I see any patterns in the activities that I have undertaken in the past?
- What are my weaknesses?

This last question is especially important to address. You will want to be able to speak frankly about your weaknesses as it will demonstrate that you have an awareness of your limits and that you have a clear desire for self-improvement. Such qualities are essential for any interviewee but especially for a counselling candidate as they are the foundational characteristics of an effective and professional therapist. Do not be afraid to address these issues in an interview if asked. Candid discussion of 'weaknesses' help to illustrate a confident and relaxed individual.

In addition, if you have undergone personal therapy yourself, you will want to reflect upon that experience. Ask yourself, 'What did personal therapy teach me about myself and how will this help me as a counsellor?' Such reflection will help you to speak about who you are, rather than just what you do. You need to find a balance and speak about both these aspects of yourself. For instance, you may want to mention your work as a volunteer at a children's hospital but then you will also want to discuss how such work has developed you as a person. Spell it out for your interviewers. Don't make them read between the lines because in most cases they won't. Your interviewers have too many people to see to analyse each individual in depth. The more you give them up front, the more defined as an individual you become, and hence the more they will remember you. That, remember, is one of your primary goals.

THE BIG SELL

Now that you have thought about you, you need to think about how to 'sell' you. To continue with our analogy above, if you were selling your car you would cater your sales pitch according to the individual. To a 25-year-old college student, you might stress how much fun the car is to drive, to a mother of two, you might emphasise the safety features, and to a part-time carpenter, you might highlight the large boot space. Likewise, you will want to cater your sales pitch of you to the particular college you are approaching. You need to think like a 'buyer' – in this case the college. For instance, at a college that values academic achievement above everything else, you might want to expand upon your educational achievements, whereas at a school that values diversity you might want to highlight your studies abroad.

At any school, however, certain aspects of your 'sales pitch' will remain the same. All colleges offering counselling courses will be looking for certain qualities in their candidates that will be assessed not only from your background details but also from your behaviour and answers during the interview. These will include:

- good listening skills;
- the ability to judge and adjust pace;
- a flexible nature;
- the skill to handle confrontations;
- positive body language;
- a responsiveness to feedback;
- confidence;
- the ability to interact with a broad range of people;
- quick thinking skills.

An interviewer will not only be assessing your technical knowledge, intelligence, motivation, and interest in the course, but she will also be taking note of your communication skills and overall common sense. This is why you will want to have studied yourself beforehand. Only someone well aware of his strengths, weaknesses, skills, abilities and history will be able clearly and skilfully to articulate under such conditions.

Interviewers will also attend to how you deal with ambiguity and problems that do not have a definite solution. They might want to see how you respond to criticism or praise and may ask questions that challenge you to think quickly and creatively. In a group interview, they may set up scenarios or role plays to assess your ability to work with others, communicate clearly, motivate others, and respond to differing viewpoints. They will respond positively to someone who is flexible and reasonable while they will be discouraged by someone who demonstrates rigid beliefs and a closed personality. Therefore, before any interview, you will want to practise and encourage these qualities in your answers and overall demeanour.

To do this, you will want to demonstrate a comfortable balance of confidence. You need to appear convincing with your answers but also at ease with differing opinions. A good counsellor has a strong belief system but is able to adjust his or her approach according to the needs of the client. He or she is also able to accept the beliefs of others even if they differ radically from his own. As a counselling candidate you will want to create a similar image. You will want to be focused in your answers without sounding closed to different perspectives. For example, if you are asked for your preferred theoretical viewpoint you might answer:

> I have had a lot of exposure to the cognitive-behavioural school of thought and so this is, at present, the orientation with which I feel most familiar. I like its structured approach and its strong empirical base. However, I would like the opportunity to explore some less directive orientations as I think such study would help to me to appreciate the emotional world of clients more fully.

This answer is both confident and open. It demonstrates the speaker's preference and technical knowledge. Moreover, the ideas are clearly expressed and the language is positive. The speaker is precise with his or her desires. Instead of couching his or her views with phrases such as 'I think I might' or 'I kind of prefer', he or she states them with confidence – 'I have' and 'I like'. This not only shows intelligence but careful forethought and interest. The speaker's desire to 'explore some less directive orientations' also reflects an openness to learning and an awareness of limitations. These aspects of the answer allow the speaker to appear confident without seeming presumptuous. Thus, the candidate has done a good job of balancing knowledge with humility.

When trying to strike this balance, you might find it helpful to think like the interviewer. He wants a candidate who will positively reflect on the college as a student. He is not looking for a candidate who thinks she already knows everything or who is unreceptive to new ideas. Remember, the interviewer is not your opponent. In fact, you and the interviewer have extremely compatible aims: he or she wants to find a candidate appropriate for the school and you want to be a candidate appropriate for the school. Thus, in a sense, the interviewer is 'on your side'. He wants to see your special qualities – it will make his or her search easier and shorter.

COPING WITH ANXIETY

If you are feeling anxious about the interview, remember that this is entirely normal. You may want to try to focus that energy into excitement by visualising yourself succeeding in the interview. Close your eyes and imagine yourself entering the interview with confidence, responding to questions with ease, asking questions with enthusiasm, and departing the room gracefully. You will find it hard to achieve what you cannot at least imagine – so constantly imagine yourself doing well in the interview. Remember, the interview is a type of performance. Just as you would practise for a stage production, you will want to practise for your performance in the interview by imagining yourself at your best. The more you visualise the positive possibilities and become familiar with the interview process through your imagination, the less anxious you will feel.

Reducing your anxiety with creative visualisation will also help you approach your interview with a sense of purpose and with the belief that you can achieve an offer of acceptance. Any ambivalence that you have about your abilities will be reflected in your answers, and hence your interviewers may also begin to feel ambivalent about you. You are best to remain positive about yourself no matter who else is up for a place or how difficult the school appears to be in its acceptance process. Your positive attitude will not only show interest and enthusiasm, but will also help your interviewers to feel positive about you.

THE INTERVIEW

Every interview follows a basic structure. Each will have an opening, question time directed at you, question time where you ask the questions, and then a closing process. From your viewpoint, you will want to think of the interview as having two additional elements: a preparation period just before the interview and a review process after the interview is over.

Preparation

As discussed above, you will want to arrive about 15 minutes before the scheduled start of the interview. This is so that you have ample time to prepare yourself for the meeting. Remember, a good interview starts way before you enter the interview room.

First, find the nearest washroom and double check your appearance. During your journey, your hair may have been messed, lint may have gathered on your suit, or your make up may have smeared. These are all things that will distract your interviewers.

Second, take some time out to review the things you have prepared. Think about your best qualities and the image you are hoping to portray. If you have prepared a list of questions for the interviewers, remind yourself of what they are. Brief yourself with names and departments with which you should be familiar. Take your time in reviewing these things, rushing now will only make you feel anxious.

Third, put any reminder notes away and try to clear your head of thoughts about the interview. You may wish to do this by looking at yourself in the mirror and giving yourself a quick mental pep talk. At the very least, take a nice deep breath and slow down. Anxiety will often cause people to feel rushed and pressured. Counteract this by consciously slowing yourself down and then close your preparation time before you leave the bathroom. Once outside that door you will want to have your mind clear and relaxed.

When you are finished with your preparation, find the appropriate person to confirm your arrival. Give him or her your name and the allotted time of your interview. Resist the temptation to pull out your notes and go back over your list. A rushed overview will only make you feel confused and most likely will increase your anxiety. Try to keep your mind clear of interview matters so that you are prepared to make a poised entrance.

Opening

When you are called in for your interview, try to think of the impression you want to make as you enter. You will want to walk with your head held high and make eye contact with the interviewers. Shake hands only if you are offered and then take your seat. Try to minimise any shuffling or prolonged hesitations in doing this. Once seated, wait for the interviewer to start the proceedings. If it is a panel interview, you will be introduced to the members of the panel and if it is a group you will probably spend the first few minutes with introductions of the other candidates. In both cases, try to attend to the names and positions of those to whom you are introduced. It will demonstrate your interest and an ability to listen – both key qualities for a counsellor. After introductions, the main interviewer will probably explain the structure of the interview and then proceed to the main task of asking you questions.

Questions from the interviewers

When answering questions the most important thing you can do is listen. Concentrate on what is being asked and try not to let your mind race ahead to think about what will come next or why the question is being asked. Your job is simply to clearly and confidently answer the questions addressed to you. To do this you will need to keep focused and to keep your mind on the present. If you are not 100 per cent sure about a question, do not hesitate to ask for clarification. Asking for such additional information only suggests that you have a keen desire to answer a question well. Always take your time with answering and keep to the point. Only answer one question at a time, particularly if you are in a group setting. You will want to be conscious of your place within a group and refrain from dominating the conversation.

Several types of questions may be asked of you during the course of an interview. Each is searching for particular information and you will want to formulate your answers accordingly:

1 *Open*: these questions are asking you to provide a full picture for the interviewer. They are asking you to 'tell a story'. For instance, 'Tell us about your experience as a volunteer at the women's shelter' or 'How did you find working as a research assistant?' With these questions, the interviewers are looking to get a richer sense of you.

2 *Closed*: closed questions can be answered in one or two words. For instance, 'How many years did you work as a research assistant?' or 'Did you like your volunteer work?' However, although these questions can be answered briefly, you may also wish to add details if you feel the interviewers are looking for more than just a clarifying detail or two. For instance, with the questions above, you might answer 'five' to the first question and then detail how your work progressed during that time. For the second question you might provide some details on why you enjoyed your research work. Use your judgement as to how long an answer you want to provide. but keep in mind that the purpose of an interview is to gain a richer picture of the interview candidate.

3 *Hypothetical*: these questions are used to assess how you might handle a particular situation – 'What if . . .' or 'How would you . . .'. In a counselling interview, they might be used to assess your common sense and how well you can think under pressure. Take your time with such questions and remain confident. No matter how well you answer the question, composure will make a positive impression as it is essential to any counsellor.

4 *Difficult*: the thing to remember about difficult questions is that they are not meant to trick you. They are designed to make you think quickly and creatively or simply are asked without any real intention to be difficult. They just happen to be difficult for you. Whatever the case, once again, take your time and ask for clarification if you need it. Not only will these strategies help you answer the question as best you can but they will also demonstrate good counsellor qualities.

5 *Negative*: negative questions are ones that address possible 'weaknesses' in your application. For instance, an interviewer may ask, 'I notice that between the months of March and September of last year you did not list any employment or school activities. Can you tell me why?' Once again, do not look at this question as being adversarial, but rather see it as an opportunity positively to build your profile with the interviewers. With this question, you have an opportunity to eradicate any negative suspicions that the interviewers may have been feeling. Negative questions are your chance to paint a better picture.

With all these questions, you will want to keep focused on creating the right impression. Remember to speak clearly and enthusiastically, as you will want to keep the interviewers interested in what you have to say. A good strategy for doing this is to address the 'So what?' factor (Leeds, 1993). With every question, ask yourself, 'So what?' 'What about my answer is going to make it seem special?' 'Why do they need to know this about me?' Fill in the blanks for your interviewers. For instance, if they comment that the focus of your undergraduate training was in economics, don't just confirm this fact with 'yes'. Also tell them how economics contributed to your counselling skills and desires.

Questions to the interviewers

Once your interviewers have finished asking you questions, you will have the opportunity to ask them a few. The interview is really a two-way process. The interviewers are assessing you but you should also be assessing them and the course. Courses are costly and time consuming and as such you will want to know which one is best for you. A person who asks questions in an interview does not appear naive or 'stupid'. In fact, the situation is just the opposite. A person who asks questions seems interested, inquisitive and intelligent. The person who does not ask questions appears passive and apathetic.

As such, you will want to have prepared questions beforehand for the interview that will have been generated by your research on the school. You can bring a list to help you remember your questions but make sure you have placed it in an easily accessible place. You do not want to be shuffling through your bag for an extended period of time, nor do you want to pull out a piece of crumbled scrap paper. Write your questions on a good-sized sheet of paper and keep it in a safe place. Some areas about which you might want to inquire include:

- the course routine, i.e. class times and frequencies, tutorial time, required internships;
- support and guidance offered by the school;
- assessment measures and reviews;
- qualifications and experience of key staff members;
- training opportunities;
- required versus optional aspects of the course;
- areas of the course other students have found difficult;
- financial payments and assistance;
- your personal fears about fulfilling the course requirements.

In addition, you will want to ask about what happens after the interview. When and how can you expect to be contacted? Is there an additional interview process? Does the college operate a waiting list?

The closing

As the interview comes to a close, you will want to maintain your enthusiasm and positive body language. As you say goodbye, make eye contact and thank the interviewer(s) for their time. Shake hands only if you are offered and exit smoothly with the same confidence with which you arrived. You will not want to linger. You don't have to sprint out the door, but also remember that the interviewers do have a schedule they are trying to keep. Your efforts to keep them on that schedule will be appreciated. Finally, close the door behind you if you are not escorted out.

The review

Some time after you are outside the interview building, you will want to review your performance. This is usually best done at home when you have had some time to distance yourself from the excitement of the interview and where you have some privacy. A review is an essential part of the interview process as it will allow you to finalise the interview you just finished and improves your skills for any future meetings. This is not a time to chastise or reprimand yourself. It is a time to give yourself some productive and constructive feedback. When you have a few moments to yourself, review the various aspects of your interview:

- Were you on time?
- Did you maintain eye contact?
- How was your voice? Did you speak confidently and enthusiastically?
- How was your body language? Did you fidget? Did you appear relaxed?
- Did you answer the questions as you would like?
- Did you sell yourself well?
- Was the interviewers' attention captured? Did you address the 'So what?' factor?
- Did you demonstrate a good working knowledge?
- Did you ask appropriate questions?
- How well did you close the interview?
- Overall, did you create the impression you wanted?

Once you have done this, use the information to practise and prepare for future events.

SOME FINAL WORDS

Each interview is different and you will want to prepare for each one. In addition, as you attend more interviews you will also gain confidence with your experience. However, a little anxiety before an interview is perfectly natural and, in fact, good. It will help you to appear motivated and interested to your interviewers. Keep in mind that you have already succeeded in the most difficult aspect of the interview – you have actually obtained one. Many other applicants did not. As such, think positively to yourself. You have done well so far and can continue to do so. Most importantly, be yourself at the interview. The interviewers want you for their course, not a surprise. If you have to be someone else to secure a place, then the course was not meant for you. The more you fake in an interview, the less genuine you will appear. Being genuine is the key to all present, and future, good counsellors.

REFERENCES

Leeds, D. (1993). *Secrets of successful interviews*. London: Paitkus.

Straw, A., & Shapiro, M. (1995). *Succeeding at interviews*. London: Hodder & Stoughton.

9

Expectations and the Reality of Training

Kasia Szymanska

> Graduate school can only give you a start because of its inherent limitations and your own overly high expectations.
>
> (Kottler & Hazler, 1997)

To be accepted on a professional training course can engender a wide range of feelings from excitement and optimism to apprehension and a feeling of dread. These feelings, coupled with expectations of the course and personal achievement, can contribute to disillusionment with the experience of training. Often, the expectations trainees have on starting their courses are unrealistic and they may serve to hinder the trainees' personal and professional development.

To address this issue, drawing on my experience as a trainer and on feedback from trainees and tutors, this chapter considers some of the more common views trainees have on commencing training in counselling and how these match the realities of training. Also included will be a section on what trainees can do to prepare for training and to ensure their courses run smoothly.

In this chapter it is assumed that training courses which lead to a professional qualification include the following: theoretical input; training in counselling skills; emphasis in personal and professional development; the requirement that trainees be in personal therapy and complete supervised counselling practice.

SOME COMMON TRAINEE EXPECTATIONS

This course must teach me everything I need to know to be an effective practitioner

Having found and being accepted on a course of their choice, trainees are often under the misconception that once they finish their training their knowledge base will be complete.

The reality

Attendance on a training course is the first step along the path towards professionalisation. It is a rich period of intense structured assimilation and application of information. Training courses are not designed to teach trainees everything they need to know about counselling. Rather, training opens the door to further accumulation of knowledge, learning of new theories and techniques, increase in confidence and ability and ultimately professional registration. Reflecting on the transition from trainee to professional, Kottler and Hazler (1997) write: 'Each of us has to come to grips with the tenuous nature of truth, the mythology surrounding what it means to be an expert, and the vast differences between what we learned in school versus what is required of a practising professional' (p. 51). Their views are substantiated by earlier research conducted by Skovholt and Helge Ronnested (1995) into the professional development of counsellors and therapists. They suggest that finishing training can lead to the painful realisation that training does not prepare them for the demands of professional work.

Learning is continuous process and training is only a small but integral part of it. Norcross and Guy (1989), in their analysis of the experiences of ten psychotherapists, found that neither formal training nor the influence of the trainers and the coursework were considered as the most significant aspect of their professional development. Rather training experiences such as clinical supervision and work experience were viewed as more influential.

I must do well

The demand to do well, to cope with the pressures of the course and to pass assessed work and exams is often at the forefront of trainees' minds. In many ways this is understandable as students may have made many personal sacrifices to get on courses; for example, to work part time or even leave jobs to concentrate on studying. On this basis, it would be safe to assume that professional training is not entered into lightly.

The reality

Doing well is important. However, demanding to do well, for example, 'I have to succeed in all aspects of the course', can be counter-productive for three reasons. Excellent marks in assignments and exams do not necessarily make a competent counsellor. The demand to succeed maybe unrealistic and holding on to such a belief can lead to procrastination and anxiety and both these feelings can serve to block progress. It is much more helpful to think along the lines of, 'I would prefer to succeed, however if I don't it's certainly not the end of the world'. Lastly, focusing energy on doing really well and getting good marks can be all consuming and often areas of personal development and a balanced lifestyle (e.g. social activities) can become neglected. It is worth remembering that both coursework and exams can be repeated and doing so does not make the individual a 'failure', rather a 'fallible human being' who like others at times isn't successful in all aspects of their lives.

Finding a placement will be easy

A core element of training is supervised counselling practice. The number of clients whom trainees are expected to counsel and the length of contracts can vary, and often depend on the settings in which trainees work and the therapeutic orientation(s) to which the trainee adheres. For example, trainees working in GP surgeries and employee assistant programmes will probably see clients for short-term work, while trainees working in psychotherapy departments in hospitals may be encouraged to see clients for long-term counselling.

On paper, finding a placement may seem easy. However, in practice it can be an arduous, time-consuming and at times anxiety-inducing process and even when having secured a placement trainees can still come across a number of obstacles.

The reality

Some years ago when there were few professional training courses, finding a placement was easier. Now, as the number of courses has mushroomed the scrabble for placements has intensified. While many tutors do help trainees to find placements and arrange interviews, organisations now have a large selection of trainees to choose from, so competition can be fierce and an interview does not necessarily guarantee a place. Once on placement, other difficulties can arise, such as those listed below.

1 Trainees may feel undervalued in their placements. You may be asked to start seeing clients without having a proper induction.

Effectively, you will have to learn about the organisation and how it functions as you go. You may be referred to and introduced to other staff as volunteers as opposed to 'counsellors in training', which can contribute to a feeling of being undermined and detracts from your status as a professional.

2   Trainees may feel under pressure to see clients whom they do not have the skills to counsel in order to meet the organisation's requirements and the number of counselling hours stipulated by the course.

3   As trainees often only work a couple of hours a week, they may miss staff meetings and on-site training days and as a result not feel as if they are part of the team.

4   Trainees may experience hostility from paid employees who view their inclusion as a possible threat.

5   Trainees who receive supervision on site with supervisors whose orientation is different or unfamiliar to theirs may feel confused and this may impact negatively on their counselling work.

The trainers will have all the answers

A common view held by trainees is that trainers are all experts in their fields and as a result should have all the answers to their questions and whatever the trainers say is always correct.

The reality

This view was substantiated by a small study of trainers conducted by McLeod (1995) who noted that 'staff can be idealised as all-knowing experts'. Fortunately, omnipotence is not a prerequisite of the job. Although trainers should possess a bank of knowledge and experience, their role is not to 'force feed' trainees with information. The role of trainers is multifaceted, and involves providing information, giving guidance and support, encouraging individualisation, and in doing so enhancing the trainee's professional and personal growth.

Some questions posed by trainees do require specific answers such as 'Is it all right to go for a coffee with my client after the session?' However, there is no one or right answer to the question, 'What is the best way to work with a client who suffers from panic attacks?' The answer provided depends on the trainer's own experiences and their theoretical orientation. Trainers who do provide all the answers can only foster dependence, discourage individualisation and hinder learning. Trainees may then go on to mirror this process in their client work and aim to give clients the 'right' answers without considering the needs of their clients. On a more practical level, trainers may not have the answer to every question asked. I recall a trainee was surprised when in response to a question I answered, 'I don't have the answer to that question right now, however I will get back to you about that.' Reflecting back on that moment a couple of months later, she said, 'I was surprised that you didn't know, but on thinking about it, it made me realise that there is no reason why you should know everything and neither should I put pressure on myself to learn everything.'

By the end of course I will understand myself

The implicit belief held by trainees on starting training is that being on a course will lead to self-understanding. Many of you will expect to acquire answers to questions, such as, 'Why do I get nervous when I speak to my boss?' 'Why do I feel anxious when the topic of child abuse is mentioned?' Others may also expect deeper unresolved issues to be unravelled and understood.

The reality

Self-understanding does increase and questions do get answered. Skovholt and Helge Ronnestad (1995) write: 'The lives of significant others and, most of all, oneself are constantly being understood through newly acquired psychological concepts' (p. 25). However, as with the acquisition of knowledge, self-understanding and personal reflection is a continuous process. Most advanced counselling courses encourage trainees to develop self-understanding via the personal counselling route (Legg, 1999). The number of sessions required and the type of approaches utilised by the personal therapists vary from course to course and can depend on the regulations of the awarding body.

The question as to whether personal counselling is essential to trainees is contentious. There are benefits to being in counselling as a trainee. These include:

- to help trainees experience of what it is like to be a client;
- to gain insight into the process of therapy;
- to gain insight into the issues which motivated them to enter this line of work;
- to observe the therapist working;
- to utilise the time to discuss their experiences of the training.

Reflecting on their experiences of personal therapy, the psychotherapists surveyed by Norcross and Guy (1989) suggested that warmth, empathy, transference, countertransference and the recognition that change can occur contributed to their 'lasting lessons from personal therapy'. On the other hand, personal counselling while in training can have some drawbacks. First, the cost of counselling, which can run into thousands of pounds, something for which the trainee may be inadequately prepared. Second, therapy may uncover old psychological 'wounds', which can lead to a period of emotional instability. At some point, the trainee may be faced with the dilemma of whether to continue with therapy or carry on seeing clients. This could contribute to difficulties in the counsellor–client relationship or ceasing to see clients and not completing the number of hours of personal therapy stipulated by the programme. Third, finding the 'right' therapist can be hard work and time consuming (for further information on this issue, it is worth reading the chapter on 'Getting the most out of personal therapy' in Bor & Watts, 1999: 131–145). Individuals who are not in training go into counselling of their own choice and can leave if they do not find the counselling helpful. In contrast trainees may feel under pressure to stay with counsellors with whom they do not feel comfortable in order to meet the required number of personal counselling hours. At the very worst such an experience could contribute to exploitation and lead to additional problems for the trainee.

The course will slot into my lifestyle

Two questions my colleagues and I ask when interviewing applicants for courses are: 'What types of support do you envisage you will need when undertaking training?' and 'What impact do you perceive this course will have on your lifestyle?' More often than not, in answer to the first question, interviewees tend to minimise the possible impact of the course on their lifestyle and believe that the course will fit in neatly without much disruption. In answer to the second question, many say their main form of support will come from partners, friends and hopefully peers, without considering other valuable sources of support.

The reality

Very few trainees sail through their training without a hitch; in fact, it is important not to underestimate the impact of the training on lifestyle. To help deal with the strains of training, good support is essential and that can come from sources other than those already mentioned by the interviewees. In a study which focused on the sources of support counsellors required while in training, Jensen (1994) found that counsellors rated prayer, alternative medicine, workshops, personal therapy, supervision and sports as important. In addition, attendance on courses can precipitate a number of stresses. Some of the more common which arise as training progresses are listed below:

1 *Coping with time pressures.* The completion of assignments can take longer than anticipated, and it is not uncommon for ink cartridges in printers to run low and for computers to crash. Often computer problems occur just as work needs to be submitted for marking. Waiting to borrow necessary course texts from libraries can add to difficulties and, as already mentioned, finding placements for supervised work experience can often take more time then expected. In turn, managing course pressures can eat into quality time with partners, family and friends. As one trainee said, 'I've spent endless time trawling through literature articles, drafting and re-drafting work, I'm left feeling lethargic and overwhelmed by words, at this point I really find it hard to be involved with my family.'

2 *Dealing with relationship difficulties.* Skovolt and Helge Ronnestad (1995) suggest that trainees who are starting out in this field often apply their newly acquired knowledge and skills on friends. This can have both positive and negative effects on relationships. One trainee found that his training in listening and responding skills lead more and more of his friends and to ask him 'to help sort out their problems'. He felt flattered to be asked and responded to their requests with zest. Conversely, friends and acquaintances may find the trainee's application of skills intrusive and uncomfortable and can object to being 'psychoanalysed'. Partners of trainees may have difficulty adjusting to their partners' new 'roles'. They can feel threatened by the partner's new insights and worry that 'their relationship' may be the topic of conversation with the trainee's personal therapist. This can ultimately lead to difficulties in the relationship.

3 *Managing financial pressures.* Generally, courses are expensive, and on top of fees the trainees need to pay for personal therapy, supervision and books. Travel costs and childcare costs often need to be taken into consideration, as does the emphasis on personal and professional development. Many courses encourage trainees to attend conferences and workshops as part of their continuing professional development. While many organisations do charge trainees less for attending workshops, the costs can still mount up. Unless trainees make themselves aware of all the costs of training, financial problems can be incurred and these may be especially hard to deal with if trainees have families to support.

Will I be good enough?

Many trainees ask themselves 'Will I be good enough?' 'Will I be good enough to get and keep clients?' 'Am I good enough to complete the course work?' Levels of self-doubt can be high at the start of training and may fluctuate as the course progresses. Certain aspects of the course may heighten self-doubt such as: comparing experiences with peers; receiving information about course workload from tutors; giving in and receiving assessed work; starting to see clients; preparing for and sitting examinations.

The reality

Self-doubt is a normal and inevitable part of the developmental process. Belief in one's own abilities increases with experience. Skovholt and Helge Ronnestad (1995) suggest that 'Accumulated Wisdom is a major factor in the reduction of angst. Often knowledge produces expertise and therefore the reduced angst' (p. 116).

While some self-doubt is normal, pervasive self-doubt can have a negative impact on the trainee's progress. For example, trainees who believes they are not good enough as counsellors would find it hard to work with clients' low self-esteem. Likewise trainees who do not believe they are good enough may blame themselves when clients drop out of counselling, instead of accepting that it is commonplace for clients not to finish counselling. Trainees who tend to doubt their competence on a regular basis would probably benefit from discussing their concerns with a counsellor.

WHAT TRAINEES CAN DO TO IMPROVE THEIR CHANCES OF SUCCESSFULLY COMPLETING THEIR COURSE

Issues to consider prior to starting training

Most of the *questions* trainees have about their courses will probably have been answered during their interviews. However, due to 'interview nerves' or lack of time some interviewee questions may remain unanswered. At this point, trainees may either telephone the tutors for further information or ask to speak to current or past trainees about the course. The latter is recommended because it gives trainees a 'trainee-centred perspective' on the course.

Many tutors send a core *reading list* to trainees prior to registration. There are a number of benefits to reading some of the texts recommended before commencing training. It helps to reduce reading on the course, broadens knowledge of topics to be covered on the course and can serve to reduce levels of stress once in training.

Trainees are encouraged to start making *placement enquiries* as soon as they are accepted on the course. Unless you are expected to gain experience working with a specific client group such as children, it is preferable to look for placements that provide counselling for individuals with a variety of problems, for example, relationship difficulties, depression, stress and anxiety, as there is time to specialise later. If trainees are already working in a counselling setting, it may be possible for their current employers to provide them with an appropriate placement. If not, trainees can send out their CVs together with a covering letter to organisations such as GP surgeries, NHS clinical and counselling departments and voluntary agencies.

Trainees are also encouraged to start looking for *personal counsellors and supervisors* before their courses begin. Depending on the organisation that accredits the course, e.g. British Association for Counselling and Psychotherapy (BACP) or United Kingdom Council for Psychotherapy (UKCP), some may specify that trainees seek counselling from and find a supervisor who is registered and/or accredited with these organisations. If this is the case finding a counsellor and supervisor can be more difficult, especially for trainees who are unable to travel far or live in rural areas. Trainees should consider ringing the accrediting bodies to ask for a list of counsellors/supervisors in their areas. To make the process easier, before contacting any counsellors or supervisors, trainees can ask themselves the following questions:

- Do I want a male or female counsellor/supervisor?
- How much can I afford to pay?
- Would I prefer to have group counselling/supervision? (This may depend on course stipulations.)
- What is the counsellor's/supervisor's theoretical orientation?
- When would I be able to fit in the counselling/supervision (e.g. daytime or evenings)?
- What do I want from supervision (e.g. to deepen my understanding of my current approach, to learn about other approaches or to develop new techniques)?

Trainees should ensure their *support systems* are firmly in place before the beginning of the course. Life stresses coupled with the stresses of training can lead to burnout. If, as a result of work or other pressures, trainee support systems have been neglected, they should consider making a list of the support they would like and then aim to include both emotional and environmental support into their schedules. Individuals who provide emotional support include friends, professional colleagues and family who can listen and help trainees put their problems into perspective. Environmental supports are designed to improve quality of life and include short breaks, hobbies, evening classes, country walks and going for meals (Milner & Palmer, 1998).

Issues to consider when in training

Time management skills need to be put into practice, including:

- prioritising work in accordance with course deadlines;
- working on one piece of course work at a time;
- leaving time for the unexpected, e.g. computer problems;
- setting aside time for preparation or thinking;
- not procrastinating.

Trainees who do procrastinate may benefit from the following exercise. Imagine yourself starting to do the work you put off doing regularly. Do any thoughts or images come to mind? For example, the thought 'this is going to be such hard work', or an image of yourself sitting in front of the computer struggling to write the first sentence, not knowing where to start. Try to identify all the thoughts/images, which may be stopping you from beginning the work, and then focus on changing these images and challenging the unhelpful thoughts. Imagine yourself sitting at the computer feeling relaxed and thinking 'I can do this work'. Work at challenging any unhelpful beliefs and if you choose to use imagery practise picturing yourself writing on a regular basis. Above all, set aside time each day or week to do the work, and don't forget to reward yourself for all your hard work.

Trainees should use the *tutorial support* available. Any concerns about work, meeting deadlines or personal worries can be discussed with tutors. Tutors do understand the difficulties involved in training, both from professional and personal experience – after all, they were once trainees themselves.

CONCLUSION

The ideas presented in this chapter are designed to encourage trainees to consider and reflect on the impact expectations may have on their personal and professional development while in training. The expectations discussed, together with the realities, which are by no means absolute or exhaustive, are intended to assist trainees to deal with the challenges of beginning training.

The perspective that training wholly prepares the counsellor intellectually, emotionally and practically to work effectively with clients is misleading. Rather, training is the first important rung in the ladder of professional development. It paves the way for new challenges such as developing a style of counselling which does not necessarily follow the model(s) taught in training, developing skills to counsel specific client populations and on a practical level finding work in the field.

REFERENCES

Bor, R., & Watts, M. (Eds) (1999). *The trainee handbook: a guide for counselling and psychotherapy trainees.* London: Sage.

Jensen, K.H. (1994). The stresses of counsellors in training. In W. Dryden (Ed.), *The Stresses of Counselling in Action.* London: Sage.

Kottler, J., & Hazler, R.J. (1997). *What you never learned in graduate school: a survival guide for therapists.* New York: W.W. Norton.

Legg, C. (1999). Getting the most out of personal therapy. In R. Bor & M. Watts (Eds), *The trainee handbook: a guide for counselling and psychotherapy trainees.* London: Sage.

McLeod, J. (1995). *An introduction to counselling.* Buckingham: Open University Press.

Milner, P., & Palmer, S. (1998). *Integrative stress counselling: a humanistic problem-focused approach.* London: Cassell.

Norcross, J.C., & Guy, J.C. (1989). Ten therapists: the process of becoming and being. In W. Dryden & L. Spurling (Eds), *On becoming a psychotherapist.* London: Tavistock/Routledge.

Skovholt, T.M., & Helge Ronnestad, M.H. (1995). *The evolving professional self: stages and themes in therapist and counsellor development.* Chichester: Wiley.

10

Getting the most out of Training

Malcolm C. Cross and David Glass

Candidates in psychological therapies will engage in learning through a range of teaching modalities. This chapter sets out to review and discuss some the most common events encountered as you negotiate your way through the training enterprise. It has been written collaboratively by a trainee and a lecturer in counselling psychology and psychotherapy and hopefully represents an informed and balanced view on the topics covered. Our intention is not to give hard and fast rules but rather to offer suggestions that aim to maximise your learning experience whilst in training. This chapter is divided into nine subsections that are associated with training and includes an account of learning activities that take place within and outside the university or institution of professional training.

PARTICIPATING IN LECTURES

As lectures are the context in which much of the course material is presented to members of a particular course, groups may be large, the format may be tightly structured and the presentation mode formal. On first sight, therefore, the title of this section might seem to represent somewhat of an oxymoron. This is only so if you view being in the audience of a lecture a passive activity. Indeed there is probably no less successful formula for learning than the notion of the active lecturer and the passive learner.

Active listening is critical if you are to gain the maximum benefit from a lecture (Ross, 1996). As a student in psychological therapies you will appreciate that there is a more to listening than hearing. Listening involves 'attending' and there are many more impediments to attending than your physical capacity to hear and the audible qualities of the presentation. Attending is about making active sense of the material and not allowing yourself to be distracted by what is happening around you or by intrusive or otherwise disruptive thoughts. Lectures are not times to write lists of things to do or plan future social activities. By dividing your attention or allowing yourself to be distracted you are unlikely to do the best service to the tasks you simultaneously try to complete.

Most students take notes during lectures and this is an important way in which you can become actively involved in the material being presented. It is important not to try to write everything down. Not only would this be near impossible to do well but it would also preclude you from reflecting on what is being said or presented. It is through your selecting the major points of the discussion worthy of note that you begin to form your understanding of the material. Your notes can serve as both an aide memoire and a reference point from which you can embark on independent reading and private study. Notes can also provide you with a symbol of progress and evidence of the work you have done. As such, they can be a boost to morale. However, they are of limited utility as a trophy of achievement if left to collect dust, undisturbed by active revision or pointers to further reading.

Where time permits it is always advisable to do some preliminary reading before a lecture. This investment yields benefits in terms of increasing familiarity with core concepts and provides you with a sense of validation in your own scholarship. If you view a lecture as an opportunity for course leaders to flag up important issues, then it is not surprising that some students often feel overwhelmed by the sheer bulk of material covered. Preliminary reading, as with supplementary reading, can help render complex concepts digestible while providing a sense of security through knowing where to go after the lecture if you want to consolidate your knowledge of the topic under discussion.

Asking questions of lecturers or course leaders is an important part of academic study. Lecturers have differing preferences in terms of when and how they will elaborate and clarify key points in the material. Typically, a lecturer will invite questions or check under-standing at key points in their presentation. Contrary to popular opinion among some students, lecturers are people too, and as such they can be anxious performing in front of a large group. As a result they may prefer to take questions at the end of a session. If this is the case then you should note your question so you can refer to it at the appropriate time. You should never assume that you are the only one not to understand what has just been presented. Student anxiety regarding the view taken of them by fellow students and lecturers can get in the way of their learning if they fear appearing foolish for seeking clarification (Papadopoulos & Cross, 1999). Managing your anxiety and actively challenging personal insecurities that can get in the way of your learning is an issue that will be discussed more fully in the context of learning in seminars and tutorials.

SEMINARS

Seminars are small group discussions usually attended by the leader or a member of the teaching team of a course. These meetings are typically devoted to the discussion of a topic relevant to that particular course. In this setting theoretical concepts are elucidated through the use of clinical or practical examples. The course team usually set the agenda for these meetings and students are informed in advance. Seminars often follow on from a more formal lecture although their content may differ significantly in terms of focus and application of the ideas discussed in lectures.

Sometimes one or more students are allocated the responsibility of leading a seminar on a particular topic. This teaching strategy has become increasingly common as institutions of higher education seek to equip students with a range of transferable skills. Not only is it hoped that students will grasp key concepts and share their knowledge and understanding with their peers, but also, in this case, demonstrate the transferable skill of preparing and delivering an oral presentation.

Everyone is encouraged to contribute to discussion within seminars. Each participant in a learning group has a responsibility to work toward creating and maintaining an optimal learning culture. An optimal learning culture is one in which learners are prepared to take risks and test their knowledge, where they are able to recognise and act on their own learning needs and are respectful and supportive of the needs of others. Seminars can help you become more at ease with performing in public and being at ease with people from different backgrounds. It may be the venue rather than the activity that can appear initially unfamiliar to new postgraduate students. Group discussions are often commonplace in the everyday learning that goes on throughout our lives. We should not be put off by the context of the academic institution. The context of the university or training institution should encourage rather than stifle your input.

Seminars are intended, among other things, to encourage critical analysis of the course material and promote debate on issues arising from the course. In seminars students can learn to speak 'academic' language and structure arguments which are both defensible and comprehensible to others. As Nortledge (1993: 57) says, 'the whole point of studying is to be able to take hold of ideas and put them to work for you'. Although in the end the most exacting way of doing this may be in writing, seminars can provide an important first opportunity to experiment with unfamiliar terms and concepts and bring them to life in an active discussion (Nortledge, 1993).

Morale is an essential ingredient to successful study and seminars can provide an important opportunity for social support. The chance to learn that others are experiencing similar challenges when faced with complex material can be enormously validating. Feelings of stupidity, inefficiency or just being 'struck dumb' are the common plague of students. Learning that one is not alone with anxieties can provide great relief from insecurity (Papadopoulos & Cross, 1999). Group contact, however, is no panacea for despair. Contact with others with whom you share the same fears and anxieties may lead to the conclusion that this shared view is the only valid perspective. Anxiety in this context can amplify. Effective groups will do rather than just commiserate. Doing in this context is about sharing or inventing strategies for coping and generating plans for action. Collaborative, action-orientated seminar groups take responsibility for learning and will rarely get stuck when faced with a challenge.

TUTORIALS

Tutorials can take a variety of forms. They are usually less formal than seminars. Depending on your training programme and institution, tutorials will have their own unique qualities. Larger institutions may divide their trainees up into assigned groups. Tutorials may involve an individual student and a tutor. Tutorials may be timetabled and/or your tutor may set aside a period of time during the week for individual students to discuss particular problems about the course with them. Tutorials are of enormous importance throughout your training. They provide a forum to maximise learning through generating ideas and providing a space in which issues and problems can be discussed. Tutorials provide a further opportunity to get to know others on the course as well as the tutor. It is often too easy, due to the intensity of work on training courses, to become isolated and detached from your colleagues. Tutorials work well when people are brought together to work toward similar goals.

In tutorials, each individual has a responsibility to create a culture that will facilitate the learning enterprise. There are no fixed formats that determine how a tutorial is conducted. It is likely however that when you first meet in your tutor group each member will be given an opportunity to communicate what they want from these meetings. If your needs are not being met, you have a responsibility to yourself to express how best you see this learning opportunity to be of benefit to you. Tutors are not mind readers and therefore rely on each student to communicate what they want from these meetings.

Tutorial groups can be characterised as groups that aim to help each trainee's learning and self-development through mutual encouragement and the sharing of ideas. It is therefore important that all members of a tutorial group trust each other. Satisfying and productive tutorial groups are often those where members are clear about the ground rules, including the boundaries of the group. Once these have been established, members can be open with each other and take the risks that are necessary in the process of growth and professional development.

EXAMINATIONS

Although continuous assessment, where you are regularly evaluated on what you are intended to learn, is increasingly been seen as a standard of good practice in higher education, examinations at the end of a course are still commonplace in many institutions. The nature, extent and importance of examinations differ depending upon course requirements and you should familiarise yourself with the planned mode of assessment. The nature of examinations can vary enormously. Some examination papers may be unseen; in such cases the student is expected to answer all or a subset of questions related to a topic. Seen examination papers are typically provided to students in advance and may be completed under examination conditions, within an institution, or issued to students to complete independently within a specified time frame. The nature of the examination has major implications for effective preparation. However, regardless of individual exam formats, one factor which may be tackled under the heading of exam preparation is that of dealing with exam anxiety.

Exam anxiety

For some students examinations, by their very nature, produce a dramatic rise in anxiety. Sometimes this anxiety has its roots in earlier unsatisfactory study experiences or it may relate to a fear of failure. Regardless of its origins, examination anxiety can not only lead to personal distress, but can also compromise your best performance. The most common approaches to dealing with examination anxiety come from the cognitive schools of therapy (Ross, 1996). Dealing with your own anxiety can give you first-hand experience of applying therapeutic techniques and completing homework in much the same way as you might assist a client with some anxiety related difficulty in your future practice. This approach to managing examination anxiety requires you to teach yourself to make helpful attributions regarding your heightened physiological arousal, to learn and apply a relaxation strategy and challenge unhelpful or inaccurate assumptions or myths associated with examinations. Some common myths about exams include that a failure will ruin your life; you have to have read and understood everything published on the topic to be equipped for the exam; and only people with exceptional memories do well in exams. Most universities and training institutions will provide workshops or printed material outlining tips and strategies to deal with exam preparation and anxiety. Failing this (no pun intended of course), if in your assessment you feel that your experience of anxiety will impede your best performance on the day, you should consult student support and guidance services within your institution or seek external professional assistance to help you manage your anxiety better. Finding creative ways to turn challenges into learning experiences will place you in good stead for the process of lifelong learning which is an integral part of becoming a therapist. Examination anxiety, if managed well, can be productive. It can provide the energy and motivation for revision and amplify the sense of accomplishment on successful completion.

Exam technique

There are well-established common failings of candidates who sit examinations. Following a review of Open University examiners' reports, Nortledge (1993) provides an excellent summary of common faults in student attempts to answer examination questions. The following provide a guide to what to do and what to avoid when responding critically and intelligently to the examination.

You must answer the question. A failure to answer the question can arise in a variety of ways, the most common probably being when candidates try to write everything they know about a topic, perhaps in the same style and format of their revision papers or lecture notes. Ask yourself if you have ever seen an examination question which read: 'Write everything you know about . . .'. It is unlikely that you have, and this is because good examinations are about much more than recall. They are about testing your capacity to demonstrate critical reasoning and show an understanding of a particular aspect of the topic. Key terms must be acknowledged in your response and links made between the question and material covered in the course. Answers should be framed so that the opening stance is objective, but leads to a logical conclusion based on evidence presented. The evidence should, where possible, differentially support several competing positions. You must avoid rhetoric and ensure that your conclusions rest on material offered in the body of your answer (Nortledge, 1993). A mindfulness of these suggestions may go some way toward avoiding the trap of failing to answer the question.

Don't be too ambitious with regard to packing your answers with names and dates. Relevance is the key and use your time wisely. Very long opening answers and answers in note form, which can be found at the end of examination papers, are the common consequence of poorly managed time. You should present your work clearly. Most notably, work must be legible before it can be intelligible. The structure of answers is also critical and there are few things as disengaging for markers than a student free-associating around the examination question. Focus your response and give it a beginning, middle and an end. Readability, relevance and reasoning are keys to examination success.

PRACTICUM

Finding a placement as a trainee can be one of the most frustrating and time-consuming aspects of your professional training. Depending on your institution, there will be varying levels of help available to you in locating a placement. It is more often the case that you are encouraged to find and secure a placement independently of the training institution. Trainees will have a wide range of previous experience. Some agencies may require that a certain number of counselling hours be completed before an applicant is considered for a particular placement. It is important to find out the individual requirements for each placement. Do your research in order to avoid the frustration and disappointment of being rejected from a setting, which was always inappropriate. It is good policy to think carefully about what aims and objectives you seek to meet through a particular placement. Selecting a placement is a two-way process, involving both you and the agency.

It is not always beneficial to pursue an area of mental health in which you have the most experience. You should perhaps encourage yourself to explore a wide variety of settings. Finding out an institution's policy towards taking on trainees and what is provided in terms of supervision and professional development will help to steer you in the right direction. A good placement is one that exposes you, as a trainee, to a wide variety of cases and provides high quality supervision. As a trainee you are providing your services for free. However, there are clearly costs for the agency in accepting a trainee onto their team. Understanding that placements have costs and benefits for both you as a trainee and the agency will help you realistically negotiate an arrangement that is respectful of both parties. It is never too early to start looking for a placement. Do your research by speaking to key people such as co-ordinators of individual treatment settings or contact qualified practitioners. More advanced trainees on your own training programme can be of invaluable assistance in providing advice and/or reflecting on pitfalls and pleasures of their practicum experiences.

SUPERVISION

There have been numerous attempts to define and conceptualise supervision. Aveline (1996) spoke of supervision as the central learning experience in training, seeing the role of supervisor as split across the functions of mentor, guide and assessor. As a trainee, your supervisor is a crucial part of your professional development. Your supervisor is the person who may contribute most significantly to your growth as a practitioner while ensuring that your practice is ethically sound and serves the best interests of the client.

Supervision is where you have the chance to reflect on your practice in a supportive environment. Depending on theoretical orientation and institutional structures, supervision can take on a variety styles. Supervision may be practised both individually and in groups. Group supervision is where there is an experienced supervisor leading a group of trainees or practitioners, enabling collaborative learning and the chance to profit from the experience of others. Whatever the format, it is a space in which skills interventions and issues of therapeutic process can be reflected upon. Additionally, supervision is a place for you to discuss the personal impact of the clinical work.

In supervision you will be asked to bring cases or examples of your practice to your supervisor for review. You may have time to discuss all the clients with whom you are working, or you may only have the space to discuss critical aspects of your work. It is important to think about which cases you are bringing to supervision and why. Dryden and Feltham (1994) caution that in deciding to take certain cases to your supervisor, you should be careful not to avoid or minimise the importance of other cases. In taking your work to supervision you are actively making judgements regarding the extent to which certain cases are more or less worrying, or carry more or less opportunity for learning, than others.

There are many other practical issues to be taken into consideration when thinking about supervision. Questions you should ask yourself include: Does the placement provide supervision? Do I have to pay for supervision, and if so, how much? What is the theoretical approach of the supervisor and can I work effectively within this framework? These are all crucial areas to think about as a trainee. Speaking to other trainees and those already qualified are useful ways to learn what to expect in supervision. Supervision has the potential to be one of the most rewarding components of your training and its impact on your professional development cannot be overestimated.

THE REFLECTIVE JOURNAL

The use of journals in the context of professional training is often employed to facilitate the trainees' capacity to reflect. The reflective journal is a personal and private endeavour. Often people tailor the way they write depending on the audience for whom they write. In the reflective journal you are typically free to write in a way which best suits you. There are no rights and wrongs. Thus, this allows you to write in your own personal style and to experiment creatively. Keeping a journal helps you to focus on critical incidents in your own development, integrate theory with your own personal experience and resolve any tensions that may arise between your developing personal and professional selves.

By writing things down, you are able to give clarity to your thoughts and feelings and allow a space in which you can generate new ideas and strategies, which will have implications for your practice. Perhaps you already keep a personal diary. If this is the case you are probably experienced in writing down your thoughts and feelings as they occur on a daily basis. A reflective learning journal need not be a whole new project – rather an extension and elaboration of your practice. The journal will be a way in which you can reflect on a variety of thoughts, feelings and experiences that occur over the period of training. When considering what to include you might examine and report upon, for example, your reactions to training and your interactions with lecturers and colleagues. It is also important to include things that you find challenging and to document how you may or may not have overcome these challenges. This may include thinking about which strategies you have attempted and how you might deal with similar situations in the future. As we progress through our training as counsellors, psychotherapists and psychologists we learn as much about ourselves as our clients. Having a private space in which to reflect about ourselves as we evolve professionally can be invaluable as an immediate learning tool and later as a personal and highly prized historical document.

There are various ways in which you can maximise the benefits of keeping a reflective learning journal. You may want to discuss your entries with other students on the course. This can be an enormously effective way of sharing experiences and generating new ideas and/or strategies. There may be times when you might wish to share extracts with a particular professor or tutor. The journal is yours and the responsibility of reaping the maximum benefit rests with you. You may by now be starting to think about how best you can make use of such a journal. Hopefully this is the case. Find a strong notebook that you like and make your first entry now.

ENGAGING IN PERSONAL THERAPY

Personal therapy may be an implicit or explicit requirement of training in counselling, counselling psychology and psychotherapy. Therapy in the context of training is both similar and different to therapy undertaken by traditional clients seeking to remedy psychological distress. As a trainee undertaking therapy as part of your training, there are some potential pitfalls that you would be wise to avoid. Knowing something of the process and practice of therapy can detract from your experience and could result in a lost opportunity for learning and growth.

One of the unique characteristics of therapy with trainees is that they may or may not present with a problem. Therapists who seek to provide personal therapy to trainees need to be skilled in working in ways that do not pathologise. Trainees too should not feel compelled to generate plausible reasons, based on their biographies, to direct the flow of therapy. It is true that all of us could identify a number of good reasons to be upset by our history, challenged by present life circumstances and anxious about the future. We also possess the capacity to live with and work through these issues in our own time and with the intra and interpersonal resources we have generated through the course of our lives. Good reasons don't necessarily make material for good therapy. Instead invitations to think about what you, as the client, would want to work on or the therapist taking an optimising view of role of therapy may be a better starting point for therapy with trainees in the role of 'client'.

As a trainee eager to know what therapy is and how it works it is tempting to be drawn into a stance of the non-participant observer in personal therapy. This eagerness to critically watch, comprehend, anticipate and construct rationales for why your therapist does what they do in their work with you will distract you from full participation. At best therapy under these circumstances is destined to become an academic pursuit rather than a unique and powerful therapeutic collaboration. At worst, this dispassioned engagement may suggest to you that therapy is 'just talk' and cause you to question the potency of this mode of helping and ultimately your career choice. Therapy is experiential and as such it demands your full attention in the role of client.

INDEPENDENT STUDY

As a trainee, you are likely to have interests that cannot feasibly be covered through your course of study. While time is of the essence, it is important to continue to fuel your interest. Don't become despondent if you are not able to have all your needs met by the structured training programme on which you are enrolled. For example, if you have a keen interest in brief psychodynamic therapy and your place of study is orientated towards more cognitive behavioural therapies there are many ways through which you can access knowledge about the topic.

The library is one of the best starting points for research. Don't be afraid to ask questions of the staff. It is important that you take advantage of the resources available and the expertise of the specialist librarians. It may seem obvious, but it is still worth remembering that the best orientation to a library is to take a guided tour. This not only provides a comprehensive introduction, but also allows you to familiarise yourself with the unique characteristics and idiosyncrasies of the particular library. Asking informed questions is the quickest way to achieving your objectives. It is important to remember that every student or trainee has equal rights to library resources. So be mindful that there will be periods of peak demand, such as around exam time. Queues for photocopiers and checking out books can be somewhat overwhelming. It is also worth noting that other students may reserve books. You should not rely on the fact that your library has copies of the required text. You should go to the library at times when you are not under pressure; otherwise it is likely to become a place that is associated with noxious experiences. It is easy to fall into the trap of visiting the library only at times of peak demand or around course deadlines. Making use of the library when you are relaxed and free of the pressure of getting to the next lecture on time or handing in that piece of course work can radically transform your experience of this invaluable resource.

In recent years the internet has become an increasingly effective resource available to trainees. The internet provides one of the most comprehensive and rapid ways to access information worldwide. It is important to remember of course that much of the material on the internet has not been subjected to the same refereeing process as published journal articles and books. Be critical of what you read. Use it as a starting point for your research and/or stimulus for the generation of ideas. Other resources worth considering are independent training courses/seminars/workshops and other libraries and bookshops. The various accreditation bodies also have journals that are published at varying intervals. In the UK the journals and newsletters of the BACP, UKCP and BPS may be of particular interest. The journals contain a wide range of articles and research studies that cover the whole spectrum of theoretical orientations and types of clinical work being carried out. Don't feel restricted by your institution's reading list. Think of it as a platform from which you can leap independently to explore an ever-expanding pool of information and knowledge.

CONCLUSION

By now you should be more familiar with a range of components commonly associated with professional training in counselling, counselling psychology and psychotherapy. Throughout our discussion of these various aspects of training you have probably noted the frequent reference to personal responsibility as it relates to the learning process. Taking charge of your scholarship is critical to your development and will not only help you negotiate your way though your structured training programme but also assist in the establishment of a pattern of lifelong learning. Your experience as a trainee should be both enjoyable and challenging.

In our chapter we hope we have encouraged you to prepare, participate and ask questions. Training by its nature provides exposure to novel stimulus, whether through new situations or course material and as such we expect it should make you somewhat anxious. Managing your anxiety and availing yourself of the supports and resources of the training institution will enable you to make the most of your learning opportunity.

REFERENCES

Aveline, M. (1996). The training and supervision of individual therapists. In W. Dryden (Ed.), *Handbook of individual therapy*. London: Sage.

Dryden, W., & Feltham, C. (1994). *Developing the practice of counselling*. London: Sage.

Nortledge, A. (1993). *The good study guide*. Milton Keynes: Open University Press.

Papadopoulos, L., & Cross, M.C. (1999). What do I do if? Questions commonly asked by trainees. In R. Bor & M.H. Watts (Eds), *The trainee handbook: a guide for counselling and psychotherapy trainees*. London: Sage.

Ross, P. (1996). Enhancing learning skills. In R. Woolfe & W. Dryden (Eds), *Handbook of counselling psychology*. London: Sage.

11

Personal Therapy

John Davy

It is increasingly common for counselling and therapy training courses to require trainees to undergo personal therapy as a part of their overall training experience. Many courses have always encouraged trainees to seek therapy, but in recent years this has become less optional. Major accrediting bodies such as the British Association for Counselling and Psychotherapy and the British Psychological Society's Division of Counselling Psychology have set requirements for a minimum number of hours in therapy (currently 40).

For many experienced therapists whose training included personal therapy, this requirement may seem very natural. Some argue that personal therapy should be an ongoing requirement throughout a practitioner's working life, not just during initial training. However, there are critics who argue that there is no clear evidence base demonstrating that personal therapy produces better therapists. The trend towards mandatory personal therapy may also seem puzzling to people who are not familiar with the 'culture' of therapy. After all, society does not require that police officers are arrested and interrogated during their training, nor that doctors have any particular illness history or a passion for physical fitness.

I will use this chapter to outline some of the arguments which have been made for and against the requirement for personal therapy in training. My aim is to help you balance some of the pros and cons in relation to your own plans and beliefs, rather than to support unequivocally one side or the other. Towards the end of the chapter, I offer some guidance on arranging personal therapy if you do decide to proceed.

For ease of reading, I shall use 'therapy' throughout this chapter as a generic term for the 'talking therapies' variously known as counselling, psychotherapy and counselling psychology.

WHAT IS THE RATIONALE FOR PERSONAL THERAPY AS PART OF TRAINING?

Many different arguments can be made for or against personal therapy. I will structure the discussion that follows around seven different axes of debate, although there is some overlap between them. Personal therapy can be seen as a way of:

- producing more resilient therapists and/or weeding out 'weak' ones;
- developing therapist self-awareness, or self-reflexivity;
- providing experiential learning about therapy skills and processes;
- challenging the trainee's preconceptions about therapy;
- learning about the client's perspective;
- processing course experiences and integrating these with other life experiences;
- paying entry fees to an exclusive club.

Personal therapy to produce more resilient therapists and/or weed out 'weak' ones

It is widely agreed across many therapeutic orientations (psychodynamic, humanistic, existential, transpersonal, systemic, etc.) that 'the person' of the therapist and their capacity to relate to clients is a very important resource, probably more so than any particular technique (Miller, Duncan & Hubble, 1997: Chap. 4). Most practising therapists would probably agree that their work is potentially very demanding personally and at times draining, and would acknowledge that some client work places considerable strain on the therapist. This is particularly likely when clients are struggling with very distressing experiences such as terminal illness, severe domestic violence, torture or deportation. Therapists may also feel particularly drained by clients who have relatively indirect or unclear ways of communicating their needs (e.g. clients with very restricted speech, who are experiencing frightening delusions or hallucinations, or who tend to express distress through physical harm to themself or others). These strains are particularly likely to cause problems when the therapist is feeling particularly vulnerable or tired, or is wrestling with very similar personal problems.

Some theories of therapy view the experience as one of personal growth and development. For example, person-centred therapists see much of their work as helping clients to experience the world and themselves through their true 'inner' self. A presumption is made that effective therapy will help make the true self more accessible, which will in turn leave clients more resilient, and also more sensitive to their own feelings and those of others. Some psychodynamic work is seen as strengthening the functioning of the 'adult' ego state of the client, keeping in check the more irrational instincts of the id and the harsh admonitions of the superego. Conceptualising personal therapy in these terms suggests that an effective personal therapy may help the trainee to withstand the rigours of their work and draw upon deeper personal resources.

However, this can be seen as an argument in favour of 'personal development' work for trainees rather than for personal therapy as such. There are other ways of building up one's inner reserves, self-confidence and resilience than one-to-one talking therapy. Equally, there are other ways of managing stress. There is little clear evidence for or against the assertion that personal therapy really makes therapists more resilient in ways which are then also helpful to clients.

Sometimes personal therapy is seen as a kind of screening which may help prevent people becoming therapists who are too preoccupied with their own concerns, vulnerable or 'psychologically troubled' to be of service to their clients. This could happen in two different ways:

1   Some trainees may reach the decision that there are some issues in their own personal lives which need addressing before they take on the work of 'helping' others, and so postpone training. Alternatively, they may realise that their reasons for seeking therapy training could be met in more satisfying ways.

Example

Bethany was a black community psychiatric nurse in her forties who had recently completed a part-time degree and was considering a career change to become a counselling psychologist. Personal therapy helped her realise that she still enjoyed her clinical practice as a CPN, but felt frustrated by the lack of promotion opportunities available to her, and angry at the apparent disrespect shown by her managers, who were younger than her and white. She decided to put her decision to retrain on hold. Instead she adopted a more assertive approach to her next appraisal, while exploring more senior psychiatric nursing vacancies in another service.

2   The therapist may come to a view that the trainee is too troubled or vulnerable to be 'safe' working with clients, and may decide to make a recommendation to the trainee or the course about this. However, this explicitly evaluative role is one that many therapists

would be very reluctant to adopt. Most courses do not invite feedback from therapists about trainees or the personal issues they are discussing beyond confirmation of attendance.

Personal therapy as a way of developing therapist self-awareness

Many forms of therapy aim to develop greater self-awareness or 'self-reflexivity'; insight into the contribution a person makes to situations and relations in which they find themselves. It may be unrealistic or indeed downright arrogant to expect therapists to be more 'sorted out' or psychologically secure than other people. However, it is probably helpful for therapists to develop awareness of their strengths and vulnerabilities, and monitor how this affects the way they conduct therapy and attend to the concerns of their clients. Similarly, although personal therapy clearly cannot change the age, ethnicity and sex of a therapist, it may be useful for the therapist to have some insight into the ways in which these factors figure in their relationships with people who may be from very different backgrounds.

Example

Frank was a trainee therapist who said he wanted to use his therapy to explore how a long-standing tendency towards anxiety had affected his personal relationships. However, the therapist noticed that Frank would often interrupt himself and change the subject when this theme arose. The therapist helped Frank notice this tendency to 'de-escalate' anxiety-provoking situations, and make a connection to his particular interest in solution-focused therapies, which aim to work with the client's strengths and focus on desired goals. The trainee remained a relatively anxious man, but became more watchful of his tendency as a therapist to skate over the worst fears or most traumatic experiences of his clients. The change seemed helpful for his clients, who no longer felt that his solution-focused therapy was simply encouragement to 'look on the bright side'.

There are many other ways to develop self-reflexivity besides personal therapy, such as co-counselling, personal diary work, group exercises and classroom-based exploration of family/cultural histories. However, an experience of confidential individual therapy in parallel with such learning may offer a safe space in which to explore such issues in greater depth. Trainees may be able to use group-based personal development work, clinical supervision and individual personal therapy synergistically, using each to explore related issues from different perspectives.

Personal therapy as an opportunity for experiential learning about therapy skills and processes

Undertaking personal therapy during training can be seen as a way to learn more about the style and techniques of a specific therapeutic orientation, complementing learning from the classroom, reading, supervision and placement experiences. It might also be useful for a therapist to be able to call on the memory of their own therapy experience as a point of reference ('What would my own therapist have said at a moment like this?'). If one is using personal therapy for this purpose, it follows that one should select a therapist acknowledged as having particular expertise in the specified model.

Many counselling and psychotherapy training courses aim to teach one specific model of therapy, and usually require that the trainee's personal therapist also uses that model. However, some trainings offer more flexibility. In particular, counselling psychologists are required to demonstrate knowledge and proficiency in three different approaches. Some courses may offer trainees the option of having personal therapy in a style which the trainee does not intend to practise, as a way of broadening horizons.

Example

Adrian was studying cognitive-analytic therapy, cognitive-behavioural therapy, and rational emotive behaviour therapy (approaches emphasising individual rationality and conscious action). He decided that a personal experience of transpersonal therapy emphasising spiritual and trans-individual themes would add a distinctive flavour to his training. He enjoyed the experience, but remained unsure how useful it would be for his clients in a statutory setting. However, he felt that he was better placed to communicate and collaborate with the counsellors working in a local voluntary agency who were trained mainly in humanistic and transpersonal approaches, since he could 'speak their language' better.

Critics of this position have argued that there are many other ways of learning about therapy skills and processes and reflecting on one's own practice of these, suggesting in particular that high quality clinical supervision is more important. Supervision is an ongoing arrangement between a trainee and a more experienced therapist to review and develop the therapy work and skills of the trainee in relation to their casework. Some trainers emphasise the use of audio/video tapes to review counselling sessions in supervision, or 'live' supervision involving observation of the session as it happens (e.g. Haley, 1996).

Personal therapy as a way of challenging the trainee's preconceptions about therapy

I have already suggested that the requirement for personal therapy might seem odd if one compares this with the training of other professionals such as doctors or police officers. Clearly it is possible to be a good doctor without significant illness experience. Equally it is possible to be a terrible doctor despite multiple experiences of family and personal illness and recovery. This analogy holds good if one assumes that the role of therapy is to fix something that is broken, or to 'treat' problems with solutions. From this perspective, what matters first and foremost are expert technical skills of diagnosis and problem solving, with the personal qualities and relationships of the expert being of secondary importance.

Viewed in this way, it is perhaps understandable that some trainees consider a requirement for personal therapy almost an insult or critical accusation. The requirement can be heard as a suggestion that there is something wrong with the trainee which needs to be put right before they can become a therapist. Some training courses have historically used personal therapy in just this way, not as a mandatory learning experience for all trainees, but as remedial or 'reparative' action to support a trainee who seems to be struggling.

One substantial argument in favour of personal therapy as part of training is the opportunity it offers to challenge models of therapy which focus too narrowly on pathology rather than people. The trainee's personal therapy provides a space in which to experience and develop a broader or more holistic view of counselling and psychotherapy as an interpersonal or social process (McLeod, 1999), rather than a search to find and fix a client's problem by the therapist as clinical expert. This fits well with models of therapy which share responsibility for change with the client, which aim to respect the client's competencies and skills, and which see therapy primarily as a form of constructive conversation focusing on meaning, relationships and belief systems between two (or more) people, rather than a form of cognitive/psychological repair workshop.

Learning about the client's perspective

Although a personal therapy of 40 sessions is probably too brief to offer more than a 'taster' of a specific theoretical approach to therapy, it may be a useful way to gain insight into processes and skills which are common to many forms of therapy. These might include: different uses and meanings of silence; ways of clarifying what has been said; drawing connections between apparently unrelated issues; offering alternative ways of understanding or behaving; and matching pace between therapist and client.

Most therapy students hear early on about the importance of Rogerian 'core conditions' of unconditional positive regard (non-judgemental warmth), empathy (a striving towards deep under-standing), and congruence (genuineness and immediacy in the relationship). Personal therapy should help trainees understand some of the varied ways in which these conditions can be beneficially communicated, and perhaps also experience their 'hollowness' when a therapist simply seems to be 'going through the motions' (Mearns & Thorne, 1988).

Many therapists in favour of a personal therapy requirement argue that it is vital for trainees to develop their capacity for empathy with clients by having an experience they can 'refer to' of being a client themselves. For example, although many therapists claim to work 'non-directively' by following a client's lead, even a short experience as client will help the trainee therapist to notice the many subtle ways in which therapists shape the flow of conversation, and gain some insight into the emotional consequences of the inevitable power differentials between therapist and client.

Critics argue that there is some danger of tokenism or complacency here. Therapists may mistakenly believe that their experience of therapy is representative of their clients, when in fact the specific issues and experience of the client may be very different from those the therapist worked on in therapy. For example, how plausible is it that a year-long training therapy conducted between two middle-class, educated white professional males offers the trainee a comparable experience to that of a working-class Kurdish woman attending her first ever therapy session in a state of crisis following domestic violence?

Processing course experiences and integrating these with other life experiences

One common theme in the personal therapy of trainees is the attempt to integrate their experience of counselling/psychotherapy training with other aspects of their lives, such as work, family life and personal history. Trainees may sometimes feel in a position where their super-visor focuses on client work, course tutors are mainly prepared to talk about course issues, while family/friends may be at risk of growing heartily sick of too much 'therapy speak'. Trainees may find that their relationships with partners/family change during training, not only because of the time and energy that is being diverted into training, but also because exposure to clinical work and new ways to theorise interpersonal and family processes may lead to a re-evaluation of existing relationships. Personal therapy may provide a space in which a trainee can make connections between different parts of their experience and resolve some of the conflicts which can arise.

Example

Jane's counselling placement involved work with clients living with HIV and AIDS. She enjoyed the enthusiastic and intelligent supervision provided by the voluntary organisation hosting the placement, read widely and provided constructive therapy to her clients. Her personal therapy seemed a much duller experience, as her therapist was clearly less animated and excited by the drama of her work with critical and terminal illness. Jane was able to share this disappointment with her therapist. Together they were able to make some connections to recent tensions between Jane and her partner, who seemed to be growing apart and losing their previous intimacy. Therapy helped Jane recognise the need to protect her private life from infection by the drama of the HIV virus (which both bored and at times frightened her partner), and understand that healthy therapeutic work in this context includes the need to preserve 'mundane', normal life, both for the therapist and for clients.

Personal therapy as an entry fee to an exclusive club

Many trainees are dismayed by the cost of arranging personal therapy for their training. Forty hours of personal therapy at full cost with a therapist in private practice could well cost £1000–£2000, excluding time and transport costs. Clearly, it is very important to take this potentially 'hidden cost' into account when you are considering whether or not to start training or trying to choose a course. A few courses include access to some personal therapy within the course fees, but many others will view this as an additional cost for you to negotiate with a therapist acceptable to them. Some critics of recent trends in therapy and therapy training have suggested that the move towards mandatory personal therapy for trainees is a form of 'job creation' for those who have already trained, almost like a pyramid selling scheme. Many therapists in private practice derive a good part of their income from training, supervising or providing therapy to trainees.

Many skilled therapists practising today did indeed have their own personal therapy before or while training, and may assume that what worked for them will work for others. In this sense, having personal therapy may be useful simply in terms of establishing credibility with some more experienced practitioners, through its status as a kind of 'initiation rite'. More positively, it could be argued that entering personal therapy is in some sense a symbolic declaration of affinity with one's future clients, a ritual acknowledgement that the dividing line between the helper and the helped is very much a matter of circumstance and social construction, rather than a fixed division between the good and the mad/bad/sad.

ARRANGING PERSONAL THERAPY

When should you begin personal therapy?

Some courses specify that therapy must have begun before or at the time of starting the training course, in which case the question is really, 'When should you start therapy training?' Other courses may require that a certain amount of therapy is completed before a qualification can be awarded. In either case, the trainee needs to take into account how much time, energy and money they are likely to have available over the period of the proposed therapy, and what demands may arise from other personal or family circumstances over the same period.

Example

Anneka planned to start her psychotherapy training in a year's time, and wanted to start her own therapy before this. However, she became pregnant. Although friends suggested that therapy can be a good way to manage stress, she decided that it might also make matters worse rather than better if the cash needed for the new baby's nappies and clothes was swallowed up by a therapist's bank account. The course was willing to allow her to follow the first year of the programme without personal therapy.

Example

Damian began a part-time counselling psychology course with no intention of beginning personal therapy until his second year. However, his lover became seriously ill. Damian contemplated withdrawing from the course, but eventually decided to start personal therapy sooner than he had planned to have a space in which to share his frustrations and fears about the course without further burdening his partner. After a while, he realised that his partner still wanted to hear about Damian's struggles ('life goes on'). Although Damian continued in therapy, the focus shifted towards the couple's management of relationships with others in the context of a stigmatising and disabling illness.

Finding a therapist

Your choice of therapist will be constrained by a number of factors:

- where you live;

- how much you can afford: typically, you should expect to pay between £25–50 per hour for therapy with a therapist fully accredited with the BACP, BPS or UKCP – some therapists may be willing to negotiate a discounted fee;

- how far and how easily you can travel, the times at which you can meet the therapist and the times at which they can see you;

- the therapeutic orientation you wish to experience;

- the type of therapy and qualifications for therapists which are acceptable to your training institution – clearly, your choice is restricted if a course requires you to have therapy with one of their ex-trainees or a therapist using only a particular approach to therapy, especially if this is an unusual one.

You may also want to take into account a variety of different factors:

- the type of 'problems' or issues which the therapist has chosen to specialise in (including perhaps whether they have experience of doing therapy with trainees in your chosen profession);

- languages which are offered by the therapist;

- the social–cultural background of the therapist, for example, their ethnicity, class, gender and/or sexuality;

- what other relationships you have or may have with the therapist: for example, it is unethical for a therapist and client to enter into a sexual relationship, so selecting a therapist because you have met them at a conference and feel attracted to them may well be problematic and potentially damaging. Similarly, conflicts of interest may arise if a trainee seeks therapy with a staff member or close associate of the training course team. The trainee may wish to discuss problems involving relationships with other staff members but feel unsure of the confidentiality and impartiality that would be offered (Barnes, 1998).

Realistically, there will be trade-offs between these different factors and you will need to make some compromises. If you decide that it is supremely important to seek therapy with a Spanish-speaking lesbian UKCP psychotherapist who specialises in issues of gender identity using gestalt psychotherapy, you will probably have to search long and hard. Some ways to find a therapist would include:

- recommendation from a friend who has had a helpful experience of therapy;
- recommendation by a member of the training course team;
- directories/registers published by accrediting organisations, such as BACP's *UK Register of Counsellors* and the BPS *Directory of Chartered Psychologists*;
- contacts and recommendations through other organisations or groupings with whom you feel an affiliation (e.g. local rape crisis centre or women's refuge, local multicultural community forum, etc.);
- community health centres and holistic therapy clinics;
- public advertisements.

Example

Eduard wanted a personal therapist who was also black and from West Africa. He began by looking in the BPS *Directory of Chartered Psychologists*, but found the level of information provided unhelpful. However, he gathered several useful suggestions from other participants attending a one-day workshop on 'Using African folk tales in therapy' held at a local family therapy training institute.

Some health warnings

Therapy is a situation where both parties may feel vulnerable at times, and both have a right to feel respected and safe (paradoxically while taking some risks with constructing new meanings and exploring feelings). To help ensure that your experience of therapy is constructive, in all cases you should adhere to the following guidelines:

1   Check directly with the therapist's accrediting body that they really do have the qualifications they claim.

2   Do not assume that your experience of any given therapist will be the same as that of a friend or previous client.

3   Enter therapy on a provisional basis, giving yourself an opportunity (which might mean one session or several sessions) to decide if you feel you can trust and work with the therapist. The therapist may also specify an 'initial contract' while they decide if they are able to work with you.

4 Clarify financial arrangements at the outset – how much therapy will cost, how much notice you need to give to avoid being charged for a missed session, etc. Never hand over significant advance payments. The norm is to pay at the time of a session, or to settle for a month at a time.

5 Expect to be treated with respect. Be aware that you have a right to complain to the therapist, and if necessary to their accrediting body, if problems do arise. Therapeutic confidentiality does not prevent you from talking to others about your experiences in therapy. Sadly, some therapists have abusively taken advantage of clients, for example, by entering into sexual relationships with them (Masson, 1988). Remember that your rights as a trainee are no less than any other client in therapy.

6 Expect the therapist to listen carefully to what you want from your experience of personal therapy. Ask the therapist how their form of therapy might help you achieve your aims.

7 Be able to discontinue therapy when you feel the time is right. Be wary of therapists who 'find' new problems that they feel you should work on as you reach a point when you feel therapy should stop.

8 Appreciate that the therapist also has a right to be treated with respect and have their own personal safety and boundaries honoured (e.g. times when they are available for phone contact).

How much therapy is enough?

One benchmark is when you have finished the amount of personal therapy required by your training course. If you have satisfied the course requirement, are running short of time and money and do not feel that there are burning issues that you need to address further through therapy, stop at this point.

Beyond this very pragmatic suggestion, the point where you should leave therapy is very dependent on the goals that you have set for yourself in therapy. If you decided at the outset to use the sessions as an opportunity to challenge a long-standing difficulty with eating habits and anxiety in social situations and the therapy has helped produce change in these areas, a natural end point would be when you have achieved 'good enough' change with these target feelings and habits, and have some confidence that you will be able to resist or manage relapse well. In other words, therapy should cease when the problem is solved (enough).

Although this sounds straightforward, in practice different therapists tend to have different views about what constitutes enough.

Some therapies emphasise that issues should be 'worked through' until they are fully resolved and understood, while other therapies empha- sise getting people 'back on track' or 'on the way', without the same commitment to accompanying the client on the journey (Hoyt, 1995).

If you decided to treat your therapy mainly as an opportunity for personal growth and characterological change and understanding, you might want to continue in therapy for considerably longer than 40 sessions if the experience so far has felt constructive and you can afford it. However, be wary of a tendency towards perfectionism or escapism which can impel some people to become 'therapy groupies', spending decades in therapy. It is important to keep asking how much personal development is 'enough' (at least for the time being), and whether there are alternative/additional ways to meet this need besides long-term personal therapy.

CONCLUSION

I have used this chapter to outline some of the reasons for and against personal therapy as an important part of a therapist's clinical training. The existence of these competing positions is indicative of the diversity that constitutes 'therapy' today. There are some economic pressures driving steps towards 'professionalisation' and the pro- motion of therapy to the public as though practitioners agreed about best practice. However, there are in fact very considerable differences between therapists about what therapy is and should be, and how to train new therapists. This makes therapy an exciting and dynamic, but potentially confusing, career option.

The ambiguity or tension between these competing arguments may seem uncomfortable. I would like to suggest that the capacity to tolerate ambiguity, to hold a variety of different beliefs about the same issue, is an important feature for most forms of therapy. Holding a 'both/and' position ('both this and that seem important in this case . . .') will often be more helpful to clients than a premature jump to 'either/or' ('either this is right or that is . . .').

Even if you have reservations about a mandatory requirement for 40 hours of personal therapy in your training, you may also be able to make use of the experience. In some respects this parallels the position of many clients. Few clients come to therapy because they really want to for its own sake. Most come because they want to change some- thing in their lives and have not yet been able to achieve this through other means. Therapists need to be pragmatists who are skilled in helping clients make the most of imperfect situations with the oppor- tunities and resources to hand, in addition to any other more idealistic positions they also aim to further through their work.

SUMMARY

1 Many courses now require trainees to have personal therapy, particularly where these lead towards BACP accreditation or BPS chartered counselling psychologist status.

2 The move towards mandatory personal therapy partly reflects clinical consensus, but may also link with some economic pressures and a drive towards the 'professionalisation' of therapy.

3 Some approaches to therapy place greater importance on personal therapy in training than others.

4 Arguments for and against personal therapy in training include:
   - producing more resilient therapists and/or weeding out 'weak' ones
   - developing therapist self-awareness, or self-reflexivity
   - providing experiential learning about therapy skills and processes
   - challenging the trainee's preconceptions about therapy
   - learning about the client's perspective
   - processing course experiences and integrating these with other life experiences
   - paying entry fees to an exclusive club.

5 Personal therapy takes time and money and is potentially stressful in its own right. Trainees should take into account other possible demands on them when considering whether to begin personal therapy and training.

6 A trainee's choices of personal therapist will vary with specific course requirements, location and other factors. Trainees should take into account possible dual relationships with a proposed personal therapist.

7 It is important to discuss aims and practicalities at the outset of therapy, and ensure that there is some 'fit' and agreement between therapist and trainee.

8 Both therapist and trainee have a right to be treated with respect and have their personal safety and integrity honoured.

9 The end point for therapy should principally depend on the goals of the trainee, not those of the therapist.

10 What you get out of therapy will depend in part on the attitude with which you approach it.

REFERENCES

Barnes, F.P. (1998) *Complaints and grievances in psychotherapy*. London: Routledge.

Haley, J. (1996). *Learning and teaching therapy*. New York: Guilford Press.

Hoyt, M.F. (1995). *Brief therapy and managed care*. San Francisco: Jossey-Bass.

McLeod, J. (1999). Counselling as a social process. *Counselling, 10*(3), 217–222.

Masson, J. (1988). *Against therapy*. London: HarperCollins.

Mearns, D., & Thorne, B. (1988). *Person-centred counselling in action*. London: Sage.

Miller, S.D., Duncan, B.L., & Hubble, M.A. (1997). *Escape from Babel: toward a unifying language for psychotherapy practice*. London: W.W. Norton.

12

Personal Experiences of Training

Susanne Robbins and David Purves

In this chapter, we present personal reflections on trainees' experiences on different courses. Susanne Robbins and David Purves each write about their expectations and approaches to managing the demands of their training. These are presented separately below.

LEARNING HOW TO LISTEN: *Susanne Robbins*

Looking back over the past year, I cannot believe how much I have learned, how hard I have worked, or how much my life has changed in the process. It is commonplace that people are changed by learning and in a sense it is inevitable, as new people and places are experienced and new ideas considered. However, I did not expect to feel quite as 'different' when I reached the end of the course as I do now.

Training was not a completely new experience for me. After school I trained as a nurse and worked for several years in a variety of disciplines at different hospitals, all of which entailed further training. I gave up work while my children were young, and that period of 'unemployment' gave me the opportunity to reflect on my career and consider which direction I wanted to follow. While I knew that I still wanted to work in a 'caring' profession, I had become increasingly interested in the emotional and psychological aspects of human experience.

As a nurse I had frequently been confronted with difficult and traumatic situations in which I had no clear idea how best to help people cope. I found myself responding instinctively to the needs of the people I cared for, but was never sure whether my instincts were correct. Issues such as grief and loss were never formally discussed or explored, and while in many ways a level of emotional detachment is a necessity for nursing and medical staff, the 'silence' surrounding these aspects of care served to heighten my concern that I did not have the necessary skills to deal with them. I had always enjoyed the more 'basic' aspects of nursing – washing a sick person's face and hands seemed to me to be one of the most important things I could ever do for them – and because I was naturally quiet they often began to talk to me. I realised that I was a good 'listener' but I still did not know how to respond and I wanted to understand more about the human condition so that I could offer more appropriate guidance. Thus, I embarked on a psychology degree course which was to be the beginning of my search for knowledge and understanding.

Once my degree was completed, and with the children growing older and more independent, I began some voluntary and paid counselling work with charitable organisations. However, I soon realised that I both needed and wanted a recognised qualification in counselling if my career was to develop further. I also wanted to gain a clear understanding of how to work with people in the counselling situation so that the experience could be a positive one, both for my clients and for myself. Therefore, as part of what seemed to be a natural progression, I decided to take a full-time course in counselling psychology.

For me, choosing a course was fairly straightforward. I wanted to make use of my psychology degree and I wanted to take a course which was both academic and carefully structured. Embarking on a new venture such as this is never easy, but I have learnt from experience that everything is easier if you can break it down into pieces and take it one step at a time. I liked the fact that the course was modular and presented within a clear framework. I was eager to undertake a professional training, and felt that my nursing background had prepared me well for it. I must admit that I was a bit worried that a career in counselling would necessarily entail the wearing of bead necklaces and open-toed sandals, and I can happily report that everyone I have met has been perfectly 'normal' with not a bead in sight. I have now put my fears down to watching too many television comedies and films.

I knew that the course would entail academic work, 'practice' at an unknown placement and personal counselling. However, I confess that I did not really expect the course to be as demanding as it was. I was vaguely aware that I would be expected to write some essays and case studies, but I did not consider these to be a problem. I thought that the 'practice' component would be fairly straightforward, and receiving counselling sounded interesting. What I was concerned about were the role plays, group discussions and the experiential work that I expected would make up a large part of the course. I was certain that everybody else would be more confident, more eloquent, and more skilled than I was, and I was even more certain that I was going to make a fool of myself. These latter aspects of the course should not have worried me at all. Everybody was nervous, everybody was hesitant, and everybody had a great time. The tutors were, without exception, understanding, supportive and fun to work with. Role plays and workshops now feel like a natural part of learning and I look forward to them, as I believe most of the other students do. I even use role plays sometimes with my clients, some of whom have benefited immeasurably from the experience.

The academic component of the course was hard and I was not prepared for it. I wasted a good deal of time finding out about library cards, inter-library loans, computer databases and bookshops in order to get the necessary background information for the work. All of this used time that could have been used to greater effect on the assignment that I was working on at the time. In my desire to have the right information for each assignment I took to 'comfort buying', which is never a good idea (although it did give me something to talk to my personal counsellor about). I bought 26 books in the first six weeks of the course. I now regularly read four or five of them. Although many of the books are useful in their own way, I did not really need them and it would have been much more sensible to borrow the books from the library and extract the information I needed at the time. This would also have given me a chance to find out if the books were worth buying. I would advise new students to gather as much information as possible before the course starts. Join the library, explore the computer databases, find out which periodicals are kept where, and ask previous 'intakes' of students which books they really needed.

I would also encourage students to share information, to talk to each other about the course and to help each other out. It is often only through swapping ideas, lending books and articles and admitting our own mistakes that we learn, overcome problems and even have fun in the process. I don't know if I could have survived the year without our 'network', although I was more organised than some. If only the tutors knew the panic that set in on the evening before an assignment was due, with frantic phone calls around the network asking 'How many words over are you?' 'How many references have you used?' 'How *do* you draw a genogram?' And, at 11pm, 'Do you think if I go to bed now and put the alarm on for 4am I can finish the essay by 9am?'

I think that the hardest part of any counselling/psychotherapy course is learning to work with clients. I was fortunate that I had some counselling experience, but I was not prepared for how much time my placement in the psychology department of a district hospital would take up, or how much I would worry about the client sessions. I have often spent many hours the day before an appointment reading about specific conditions or running through an outline of the session, working out what I would do if I 'dried up' or considering how I might phrase a particular question. In addition to worrying before the sessions I often found myself worrying afterwards, wondering if I had got it 'right' or whether the client was feeling as positive about the experience as they appeared to be. In common with many students I found the first session with the first clients the most difficult. However, I was dreading something else that I knew sooner or later would happen, whatever I did and however careful I was.

My biggest fear was that one day a client I had been working with would not arrive, thus making a clear statement about the effectiveness of the sessions. It happened to me totally unexpectedly on a day which until that point had been going quite well. A client I had been seeing for a number of weeks did not arrive and had not left a message to say that she was not coming. I tried to tell myself that I had nothing to worry about and that clients often fail to keep appointments. However, as the time set aside for her appointment slipped by I became more and more anxious. I checked the waiting room several times in the hope that she would arrive late. I cogitated, I fretted, and I began to consider what had gone wrong in our last session.

The following week was dominated by worry. I couldn't help thinking that I had missed something vital or behaved badly in some way. I wondered whether I had been too pushy, too vague, or too obtuse to notice something obvious. My thoughts fluctuated between a conviction that I was so awful that my client could stand me no longer to the notion that something dreadful had happened. I was certain that at any time I would receive a phone call from my client's family, the police or the hospital demanding to know what I had done. When I received a message from the secretary at my placement asking me to phone her back, I honestly believed that my career was over. I was very nervous as I returned her call, only to be told that my client had phoned and apologised for not coming the previous week. She had been called away on an urgent family matter, had totally forgotten the appointment and wanted another as soon as possible.

While I worried too much on this occasion, it was a valuable learning experience. I have now learnt that there are all sorts of reasons why clients do not attend sessions, very few to do with my own actions as a counsellor. I know that I may not always be successful and that sometimes I may feel inadequate and disappointed in myself. However, if this causes self-reflection and analysis then I can apply what I learn from the experience to future sessions. The placement is an essential part of the learning process, and with supervision and guidance I can get maximum benefit from it.

Another component of the course, and indeed of many counselling/ psychotherapy courses, was the requirement to undertake 40 hours of personal counselling. This requirement is often viewed with suspicion by trainees, who find it expensive and time consuming and question its usefulness. I have to say that while I too worried about the cost, I quite enjoyed being able to tell someone else all about my problems and concerns. I was reluctant at first to disclose everything, and wondered how I was ever going to fill 40 hours with the same old issues. I was sure that by session ten we would have exhausted all subject areas and would just stare at each other for an hour. However, I soon grew accustomed to revealing all my everyday problems without batting an eyelid. It's quite nice to have somewhere quiet to sit, with someone who appears to listen without thinking about or doing something else at the same time and I'm quite sure that my family and friends were relieved to know that someone else had the burden of listening to all my worries.

I also become aware of how much I notice from the 'other side': the position of the box of tissues, the exact time on the clock, which cracks in the wall needed filling, how many plugs were loaded onto one socket and how many times the counsellor yawned, looked at the clock or closed his eyes for a moment (I must be terribly boring). These were all noted and reflected on. Personal counselling gave me the opportunity to observe, first hand, how somebody else practises and I hope that I made the most of the opportunity.

As the course progressed I only slowly began to realise that I was not only learning new ideas and competences, I was changing and developing in ways I had not expected. In some ways I felt infantilised by becoming a full-time student. I was eager to absorb as much as I could from the experience and keen to attend the lectures, finish my assignments and be a 'good' student. My image changed from that of a competent wife and mother to one of an unsophisticated trainee. I sat in the kitchen preparing food with books in front of me, and I joined in arguments with the children about whose turn it was to use the computer because I had homework to do. My husband became the lone parent as he struggled to sort out the disputes, and at last I understood why the children each reasoned that they needed a computer of their own. The children were largely amused by my change in status, but I became aware of how much my relationships with them were changing when our eldest son, then aged 15, put his arm around me one day when I arrived home and said, 'And how was *your* day at school?'

In other ways I was maturing and growing in confidence and ability. I was unbelievably busy, travelling from Hampshire to London two days a week, to my placement another day and, for the first three months, working two days a week. Every time I handed in a piece of work or had a good session with a client, I felt a huge sense of achievement. I felt as if I was doing what I was always meant to do, and I loved it. Learning in a stimulating environment with students who become friends adds to the learning experience. When considering a university course it's not easy to know whether you will get on with the other students or what the university will be like to work in. However, if you can find out about the culture in advance from previous students and it sounds good then that's a positive point.

I enjoyed every aspect of the course I chose to do, and found the balance between academic work, experiential work and 'real' practice stimulating, rewarding and fun. It was not, however, a course to be undertaken lightly. There were times when I struggled and wondered how I would cope. There were times when I felt disappointed, overwhelmed and sometimes completely disheartened. On more than one occasion I had to take myself firmly by the scruff of the neck and tell myself that nobody forced me into this. I was doing what I had chosen to do. More than anything, I want to do it well. That's what I'm striving for as I look forward to the next part of the course.

LETTER TO A PENFRIEND THINKING OF TRAINING IN COUNSELLING: David G. Purves

Dear Friend:

Nice to hear from you again. I was very interested to read that you are intending to train in counselling. I wish you well in this endeavour. As you know, I have recently completed five years of training in counselling and psychotherapy, and if you will permit me, I should like to offer some advice from that place of 'all knowing' – hindsight!

I commend you on your choice of career. If you are like me, then the decision to train will feel very significant indeed. Some things will feel like they have fallen into place in your life, but there will also be questions, and even fears, concerning the length of training and your own personal ability to succeed. I suspect in the beginning, many people have motives as confused as my own when they contemplate training: desires for personal development mixed in with vague ideas of helping people, and not very realistic views of what it is actually like to be a therapist. But if the truth were told, I needed to train for my own well-being as much as anything, to help me be more 'human' and to put me onto a path of personal and professional growth I felt I needed at that time. My decision to train came after about five years of interest in self-development, but actually not feeling personally developed enough to believe that I had anything to offer anyone else. I cannot say what changed my mind or what the pivotal point in my decision was, but I suppose like many people I could no longer find any plausible excuses for putting it off. However, when I had finally committed to train it did feel like I was in the right place for the first time.

Have you sent for a lot of information? I read the prospectuses of a number of different schools and chose one that seemed to offer everything I might have wanted as if I had written the prospectus myself. Reality is sometimes different. The quality of training can be very variable. My first year gave me tremendously important experiential opportunities, but I sometimes felt that I knew more about psychology than the tutors did (because I was keen and I read a lot). This was not a satisfactory situation given that I was paying them to teach me. If I had only wanted a strong experiential course, then all might have been well, but I also wanted to think and to use my critical faculties; after all, emotion is only one facet of human existence.

My advice to you is to think carefully about what you want to get from your training. This may sound a little obvious but I wish someone had said it to me! Think carefully about what you want to have achieved when you have finished, then ensure that the training you select will give you just that. I know that you are just beginning and you probably have only a few concrete ideas. Consequently you anticipate that it will all work out in the end. Well it might, and I hope that it does, but if it does not you are going to be dissatisfied. I know many people who are dissatisfied at the end because they did not project themselves into the future and see what the outcome of their training was going to be. I made the same mistake!

You see, I had always wanted to have the opportunity to work in the NHS and to be rather 'mainstream' in terms of the therapy I offered to clients (bear in mind that there are hundreds of different types of therapy in which you could train). My first year of training was warm and cosy, supportive and very 'huggy' but with a poor reputation among those I would eventually want to work with and so I had to make a choice between my future or stay on the course. I did the exercise I am suggesting you do, ask yourself: where do I see myself in four or five years time after the course has finished? What type of environment do I see myself practicing in and with what kinds of client problems? I asked myself these questions and changed my course after only one year. I chose my future. I am illustrating that it is possible to change your course at any time, and even take the credits you have achieved to date as accreditation for prior learning to a different school. There are even some courses in which you can design your own training to follow your particular interests then submit evidence of completion and a portfolio of work for your certificate. There is a lot more flexibility in training these days than you might think, and I recommend you explore these issues.

I know that we have not actually met yet, I hope that we do at some point, so please forgive me for a blunt question. How ambitious are you? Some people will convey the impression that counselling is *only* about getting in touch with feelings and having real relationships with people. These are fundamentally important issues, and in the beginning these things seem more important than anything else. There is already plenty of material written on that side of things, however that is only one side of it. Counselling is also a job! I think that an equally important consideration is how on earth are you going to live? How are you going to pay for your training, and will you ever get that money back? I hope I have not shocked you by talking about money in the same paragraph as talking about relationships and feelings? I know enthusiasm is vital when you are thinking about making such a large commitment, but planning in the beginning means less disappointment later.

When I started my training I was fuelled by idealism and determined to help people to gain access to some of their human potential. I still am, but after a while I realized that my own ability to help others was in no way determined by how, successful financially or otherwise, I might become. It was however a symbol of my confidence as a therapist. In short, I realized that I could be equally effective with clients while making a living or failing to make a living. This meant that making a living or not was my choice and in no way related to my profession. I had to decide to try and be successful. This sounds so obvious, and I am slightly embarrassed to even write about it, but it was one of the most important lessons I ever learnt, so I feel that in the spirit of collaboration I ought to share it with you. There are so many issues about money in therapy. You will probably experience a version of this problem for yourself. I know many trainees who have also 'been there' as we say. Some, I might add, never overcame it. Think of it this way: if we want clients to be autonomous and self-determining, do we not also have to model these qualities for them at times? Anyway, I hope I have reassured you to some extent, that ambition and money are not dirty words in counselling, but they are neglected words. I will leave that thought with you for the time being.

I know you have a relationship and I expect you are wondering how training will affect it. I have given this question some thought before answering. I am sometimes tempted to answer that it will make things rocky, because I think that is what people expect. But I don't think it is really true. I think that training will simply accentuate what is already there within the relationship. If it is rocky to start with, then watch out. If it is stable and loving, then fantastic. In my own relationship, since as a couple we are interested in growth, training has increased our vocabulary and the depth of our understanding of relationships. I think it has helped us. And it has helped to keep things interesting and moving. So a short answer would be 'you will have more of what you have got already'.

I was interested to read that you have some concerns about going into training in counselling, particularly with regard to the educational aspects. Let me share some of my experiences with you. Often courses have a lot of straightforward academic content. I suppose this is needed so that a trainee can develop a basic vocabulary of psychological ideas. But they remain dry academic materials until they become animated by experience with clients. One of the greatest joys I have continued to find in my work is when I experience moments of insight and I feel that I understand the academic and clinical material simultaneously. Let me explain further. In the beginning the academic material gave me the tools to be able to think about things in a coherent and logical way. But clients brought problems to me that seemed to defy analysis because of their complexity and duration. After a while of being confused, and despairing that I would ever know what was happening, the academic and the clinical material came together in a synthesis that was more than either alone. This is one of the most intensely rewarding experiences. It can happen sitting on a train or riding in a car, and it makes the reading and studying, the supervision and thought about a client all worthwhile. I have found that the best education in counselling I ever got was the one I gave myself. When I am presented with a client, and they have a problem I do not understand, I read about it. In effect, I educate myself. This builds upon course material, but the knowledge is specific to each presenting problem. It is practical education and the reward for taking the effort to understand is the moment of 'knowing'. Seek out these moments and cherish them.

A final piece of advice I would like to give you, my friend, is to expand your own interests in counselling. It is large field and there are many different areas in which you can develop more detailed knowledge. As you gain more knowledge about specific problems your sense of self-confidence and efficacy will grow and not only may you experience those moments of 'knowing', but you will also start to grow as an individual practitioner with a developing expertise unique to you. This will help to make links in the community and establish you within a therapy network.

Counselling and psychotherapy are somewhat unique fields in that they have a well-established body of theoretical knowledge, but also a highly developed applied discipline. This means that whenever you learn something in class you may always have the opportunity to apply it with a client. This is one of the aspects that make the whole field so fascinating. Stay fresh, keep engaged with what is effective and don't let yourself become too indoctrinated with old-fashioned views. Do reflect on your own practice and accept that you will make mistakes. I still do! If you do not blame yourself too much, and regard errors as opportunities to learn, then all will be well with you.

Good luck!

13

Life after Training

Diane Hammersley

WHAT NEXT?

Finding a job

The first step in finding the right job is to consider what you have to offer. This includes all the past life and work experience you have had, as well as your unique qualities and attributes. Will you be starting afresh or returning to old territory in a new role? It may be as difficult for other people to see you in a new role as for a former teacher, nurse or social worker to resist old assumptions and practices. There may be problems about working where you have been a trainee.

Here are some questions to ask:

1   Does the job specification match your qualifications?
2   Would you be properly paid and valued?
3   Are the client contact hours reasonable?
4   Is there adequate administrative support?
5   Does the job give you sufficient variety and challenge?
6   Are there funds for supervision and further training?
7   Do they promote continuing professional development?
8   Will you still be seen as a trainee in the place you have worked?
9   What will happen if you disagree with a senior colleague?
10 Are you now better qualified than some colleagues are?
11 Does the organisation know what counselling/psychotherapy is?
12 Is the service managed by a qualified counsellor/psychotherapist?
13 What are the hidden agendas?

Jobs in counselling and psychotherapy are still a relatively new feature of the employment scene and both counsellors and their employers are still in the process of working it out. For example, employers may assume that counsellors will be prepared to share client disclosures with other staff in the team, discuss and decide on shared approaches, whereas the counsellor may bring different assumptions about what can be disclosed and dual working arrangements. Organisations develop procedures that can impact on the value base of counselling which it may be difficult to challenge and justify. Some of the problems, which have occurred for others, are:

1   A central administrative and appointment system that may mean letters are delayed or where standard letters are used without regard for therapeutic sensitivity.
2   Telephone messages are not relayed or referred to the counsellor and can be used by clients to avoid the counsellor.
3   Senior staff who make assessments, delegate to the counsellor without considering that assessment as a mutual process has to be repeated.
4   Counsellors are on short-term contracts, which may be suddenly terminated as contracts are moved elsewhere.
5   People who have financial or managerial responsibility and a primary objective of efficiency, may decide policy without awareness of the therapeutic implications.

Voluntary work

Many trainees take practice placements in voluntary organisations, but rightly feel that they need to be paid once they are qualified. However, you may find that voluntary organisations have work which is paid where your qualifications in counselling will stand you in good stead. Continuing the link with voluntary organisations may provide a springboard from which to find a paid job. Some professional counsellors maintain links with the voluntary sector offering their services as supervisors and trainers, or on advisory committees.

Networking

Groups of counsellors may pass on information about job openings, vacancies or locums, hints, introductions and advice about getting a job. While searching for a job, and later in your career, you will need to know and be known by your peers and colleagues. Some of the people in your network may be more senior than you and may be in a position to write you a reference or recommendation. Those of you who decide to work privately will need contacts and people who will refer clients to you.

Joining a professional group

Membership of a professional organisation gives access to professional indemnity insurance, legal advice and much more. The British Association for Counselling and Psychotherapy, the British Psychological Society Division of Counselling Psychology, the United Kingdom Council for Psychotherapy and Counsellors in Primary Care, for example, as well as local organisations, put members in touch with training events which offer contact with others as well as professional development. You could take up opportunities to learn more about the profession through committee work. These organisations place advertisements in their journals for members who are interested in getting involved.

PROFESSIONAL ISSUES

Conducting oneself professionally

The move from training to qualification and clinical independence marks the moment when a practitioner takes direct responsibility for themselves and their views. You are entitled to a view and for that view to be heard, and it can come as a surprise when you realise that others may well listen. Somehow, you have to make the shift from the trainee who consults and takes advice on cases to a professional who has a unique viewpoint, who expects to be taken seriously or may be giving advice. Therefore, you have to consider very carefully what you say and write because your advice may be acted upon.

On the other hand, it may be hard to hold on to your views when the prevailing opinions are against yours and you face disapproval or surprise when you do not concur. Some of this may have occurred already, such as when clients come with a pre-set view of the kind of help that they need, often backed up by all the 'experts' among their family and friends. Questioning assessments, a diagnosis by the referrer or treatments offered by other professionals in other disciplines who have been consulted may bring you into disagreement with others. There may not be serious conflict but maintaining difference is important for your professional identity. It is a hallmark of the professional counsellor to hold his or her views confidently, respecting the views of other professionals while keeping the best interests of the client at heart.

Codes of ethics and conduct

All the main professional organisations such as BPS, BACP and UKCP have codes of conduct and their sub-systems may have guidelines of good practice for working in particular workplaces such as medical settings or with particular populations such as young people or survivors of abuse. If you work for an employee assistance programme, helpline or voluntary organisation, they too will have codes of practice or contractual agreements. Finally, employers may lay down standards of practice which are to do with quality or efficiency and the profession you have joined will seem the best regulated in the world. While these codes and guidelines are designed to protect clients and promote good practice, they may sometimes seem incompatible with each other or difficult to implement.

While it may be possible to subscribe to several codes, in practice it probably makes sense to choose a preferred one that represents the professional group you feel the strongest identity with, and to regard the others as available for consultation when they may be useful. Second, all codes have to be interpreted and applied and you will have to take into account the contextual factors that ought to be applied, such as organisational, cultural and legal issues. Third, ultimate clinical responsibility is yours since you and the client are alone most of the time and you must make judgements from the position of being the best informed. Always bear in mind that if a complaint were made against you, an investigating committee would seek your account of the events and rationale for your actions. This is where your knowledge of theory, practice and ethics and the support of your supervisor would be vitally important (Bond, 1993).

Relationships with other professionals

Other professionals need to know how to relate to counsellors, about their training, how they work, their professional codes of practice and so forth, and they can learn this best from counsellors themselves. So communicating information and the way this is done, gives other professionals a sense of what counselling is about, its values and holistic view of people. It may seem daunting at times, as if you have to sell yourself or justify your professional position, but if you are confident and non-defensive, you may find most other professionals welcoming and interested in what you have to say. Remember that you have the opportunity to influence a climate of opinion.

Liaison with referrers

Among the people who refer clients to you may be case managers, doctors, social workers or teachers, and they will all appreciate your prompt acknowledgement of the referral and that the client has made contact. If you need to give feedback by telephone or letter, keep it brief, respecting confidentiality and indicate whether you can help and how long it may take. Be aware of the temptation to make unrealistic promises, or say too much in order to make a good impression, and avoid the use of professional jargon.

Working in teams

Working in a mixed professional team is not without difficulties, but it can bring benefits from the sharing of expertise and support. It is important to anticipate problems that might result when assumptions are made without checking other people's viewpoint. Following guidelines such as these can enhance good professional relationships in teams:

1   Acknowledge similarities and differences.
2   Recognise the tendency for splitting, for example: good vs bad.
3   Resist the temptation to collude when you ought to confront.
4   Accept confrontation and challenge non-defensively.
5   Continually monitor boundaries.
6   Co-operate with existing practice and introduce new ideas.
7   Work for the team's prosperity as well as your own.
8   Stand up for your opinions, professional standing and yourself.
9   Take on responsibility and accept the authority of others.
10 Be aware of the group dynamics and the political environment.

Supervision

After completing training, choosing a supervisor for all or part of your work gives an opportunity to consider what you want from your supervisor (Holloway, 1995). You might consider the advantages of someone from the same professional background and orientation, who may be very familiar with your approach, or whether you would find a different perspective refreshing. Are you contemplating joining a group for peer supervision as well as having a supervisor who has oversight of your work? Does all or some of your work require specialist knowledge or expertise and do you need someone who can act as a mentor or model for you if you are entering a new sphere of work?

Supervision during training often has an educational focus and while you may still expect to learn from your supervisor, the nature of your relationship will be more equal. You need to agree on the time limit of your contract and whether you want an annual review of progress. It is important for you to choose someone whom you can respect and by whom you can feel valued. A good supervisory relationship should include support and encouragement as well as confrontation and challenge and how the supervisor does this will affect how a counsellor uses supervision.

Supervision is a place to discuss clients and the concerns and emotional distress they bring and leave with the counsellor. Being human ourselves, we need a chance to make sense of what is presented to us as well as an opportunity to share it and avoid being overwhelmed by other people's suffering. In choosing a supervisor, consider how comfortable you will feel disclosing your feelings, attitudes, doubts, ignorance and mistakes. This is the person to whom you will look for support if a complaint is made against you and who might need to tell you if your professional practice fell below acceptable standards.

Once you have qualified, you take responsibility for arranging for and consulting your supervisor when appropriate. Consultation does not just mean asking for advice in challenging situations, but also informing your supervisor of circumstances which you might not recognise are potentially difficult or contentious. These are some occasions when that might be the right thing to do.

Breaches of boundaries by the client

1 Excessive out-of-hours contact by telephone, dropping in, letters.
2 Clients who take an interest in your personal life, turning up unexpectedly, social invitations.
3 Frequent non-attendance, late cancellations, premature endings.
4 Stalking or harassment.
5 Large gifts, money or offers of reciprocal services.
6 Threats towards you, themselves or others.

Counsellor's fitness to practice issues

1 Inadvertent disclosure of confidential matters.
2 Not responding to messages, missing appointments, lateness.
3 Comments from more than one client about the same mistake.
4 Comments from a colleague about your health and well-being.
5 Complaints or disciplinary proceedings.
6 Ethical dilemmas and legal issues.

Boundary issues

1 Contacts from relatives or friends of clients.
2 Requests for information from third parties.
3 Security of client notes at work, at home, in transit.
4 Disclosure of client's history by others.
5 Clients in therapy or treatment with colleagues or elsewhere.

6 Employers or purchasers whose decisions impinge on therapy.
7 Concerns about the practice of other professionals.

Supervision is more than a condition for being licensed to practice. It can promote both the client's welfare and the counsellor's insights and may highlight areas for further study or training.

Continuing professional development

What constitutes continuing professional development (CPD) and who is it for? It is certainly one way to keep your competence and practice up to date, and it may be necessary to fulfil obligations to an accrediting authority, but it ought also to be for the benefit of the practitioner. So it should be valuable and enjoyable for its own sake, not a dreary or boring task that has to be endured. This is especially important because CPD takes time and requires effort and money.

Employers may provide training, which is a requirement of the job, and may offer access to voluntary courses that you can apply for. In addition, it is worth asking whether your employer has a budget for your training and how much that is, so that you can apply for courses and conferences outside your employment. Otherwise you have to pay for this yourself and if you have any part of your work that is self-employed, some CPD may be tax deductible.

It is not usually money well spent to attend whatever seems to be around when you are free or is within easy travelling distance. This can lead to a hit-and-miss approach, which may result in more misses than hits. Structuring your CPD so that you have a coherent strategy, which is balanced between short and longer term courses and uses a variety of methods is likely to keep you informed, enriched and enthusiastic. Aim to address your weak points and enhance your strengths.

Broaden your skills and experience

Your initial training may have equipped you to work within a particular theoretical model and you may feel confident working in a particular setting. CPD gives you an opportunity to extend your training to meet the demand for counsellors with a broad range of skills. You might consider the following:

1 *Therapy*: brief, long term, time limited.
2 *Clients*: couples, groups, families.
3 *Variety of clients*: ages, cultural backgrounds, ill health.
4 *New settings*: general practice, workplace, community centre.

5 *Learning to be a supervisor*: individual, group.
6 *New areas*: educational, sexual problems, substance misuse, psychodrama, art therapy, dream interpretation, journalling.

Methods

Your first thoughts may lead to attending short courses, lectures, workshops and research presentations, or taking advanced training and higher level qualifications. However, there are some other things that you can do regularly and on your own, such as reading books, journals and newspapers, library searches and joining internet discussion groups. In addition there is much to be gained from attending professional meetings, conferences, peer groups and networks, or engaging in committee work, giving talks and writing articles. Use a variety and what works best for you.

Experience will show you some of the pitfalls to avoid and listening to other people's comments may help to avoid large or expensive mistakes. The marketing material may exaggerate the benefits of courses and workshops, so consider whether you will be getting value for money and whether going to listen to well-known names is as useful as taking part. Beware of the temptation to attend because it is free, going because other people do, or going through the motions to get 'brownie points'.

PERSONAL ISSUES

Burnout

Before you can take care of others, you must first ensure that you are taking care of yourself, and that is one of the purposes of counselling or therapy during training. But in order to avoid burnout, staleness, feeling overworked, unable to let go, intolerant, cynical, depressed, overwhelmed, or inappropriately self-disclosing, you have to continue to take care of yourself. For some people that may mean responding to the suggestions of colleagues or supervisors and re-entering a period of therapy, if your personal life is stressful for a while.

Some counsellors and psychotherapists regard being in individual therapy or a self-development group as a way of preventing burnout. Burnout results from a mixture of boundary issues in the workplace and personal dynamics (Grosch & Olsen, 1994), so both supervisors and personal therapists may have a role to play in helping you to resolve it. When the problem occurs, you may be unable to recognise the necessity for some more personal work, so deciding now, as you finish training, that you will seek counselling if you get the nudge, is a responsible and mature thing to do. You may have to stop seeing clients for a while in extreme cases.

Living your own life

You need to live your own life, not just live vicariously through others. Helping others may give you a meaning but it is unwise and unsafe for that to become the only meaning. It really is a case of practising what you preach, and making sure that you have strong personal relationships through family and friends outside the therapeutic settings in which you work. Hobbies, pastimes and holidays are what we prescribe for others, so applying that discipline to ourselves first makes good sense.

Being a counsellor may have an impact on your personal life in a number of ways. Carrying other people's distress and suffering is in addition to what you may have to carry for yourself or your family. Fears about inadvertently meeting clients elsewhere may make you cautious about your private life so you may have to discuss this possibility. Someone may approach you for advice even when you are off duty, but you will still be responsible for its impact. Members of your family may meet clients in another context without being aware of it, threatening your privacy.

Instructions for absence

Counsellors planning to be absent should give good notice or make other arrangements for clients but unplanned absences do occur and should be considered from the outset. There are two main occasions when other people may have to act in a therapist's absence. First, the counsellor may be involved in an accident or be taken ill suddenly, and second, the death of the counsellor. The context of the work may influence who does what, since an employer or manager can check diaries, notify clients, or make arrangements for cover during absence. If there are private clients, someone has to act for the therapist to notify them too.

It may be desirable to leave written instructions or a professional will, or to decide who will act as a temporary executor of a private practice and in what ways (Traynor & Clarkson, 1996). Even therapists who are employed may not realise that there are professional matters which might need attention. Confidentiality can be maintained after the death of the therapist if colleagues or executors know what to do.

Apart from the clients' names, addresses and notes, you should consider how to maintain confidentiality or dispose of tapes, reports, case studies, diaries, files, computer records, invoices and accounts. Confidential material might also include notes on trainees and supervisees, examination questions, papers or results and documents originating elsewhere which may need to be returned. What is to happen to the counsellor's library of books, journals and magazines? It is particularly important to identify materials that are being used in collaboration with other people for writing, teaching or research purposes and that these are not automatically disposed of.

There might be any number of people who need to be informed of a counsellor's absence, depending on the workplaces and whether the absence is temporary, short- or long-term or permanent. Some of this may be the responsibility of a manager or employer who should be told as soon as possible. Otherwise, the counsellor's clients, supervisees, supervisor, therapist, colleagues, collaborators, and referrers might be contacted. Acting as an executor after a counsellor's death could also include informing insurers, professional bodies, accrediting organisations, editors and publishers.

EXPANDING HORIZONS

Research and writing

Counselling research provides a way to reflect on practice and develop theory as well as being intellectually stimulating (McLeod, 1994). You could take courses that teach research skills by way of preparing students to present dissertations and theses. Masters and doctoral courses in counselling, psychotherapy, and counselling psychology could all be avenues to pursue. These courses offer an opportunity to learn about qualitative and quantitative research methods. Books, journals, computer software and the internet provide further resources for learning about research.

Another way to develop research skills is by offering yourself as a research assistant to an existing researcher or team, who may provide training on the job. These opportunities are mostly found in academic settings, psychology departments, social service and multidisciplinary teams, clinical audit and counselling provider organisations. Alternatively, you could consider collaboration with someone else who shares the same research interests, by searching the BACP Research Network or responding to letters in journals.

One important responsibility of the researcher is to publish their findings in academic journals where they will be subject to scrutiny by peer review, thereby inviting the academic community to reflect on them. Some research training courses teach people how to write for publication, but there is no better way to learn than from reading editorial guidelines, asking colleagues for advice and feedback, and practice. It is probably better to aim to be clear rather than impressive, and your work needs only to contribute to a collective body of knowledge, not be earth shattering.

Presenting a paper

Presenting your research findings at conferences is an opportunity to practise stating your ideas with clarity and responding to the feedback from other people. It is not as easy to do this well as it sounds. A common mistake is to try to cover too much material in the allotted time, which means rattling off the words or mumbling into your notes. Your paper will be better understood if you avoid the excessive use of jargon and acronyms and do not attempt to describe complex systems verbally with elaborate arm waving. If you are using overhead slides, do not stand in front of the screen reading them out, or remove them before the audience has time to read them. Simplistic headings are just as irritating as tightly packed slides in small, faint print.

A useful rule of thumb is to aim to make 20 points in a 20-minute talk, with a brief introduction (paragraph) to set the context. Use overhead slides sparingly for visual information, with no more than eight lines of text in a large print font. Avoid colours unless the slides, projection equipment and auditorium are of a very high quality. End your paper with a brief summary of your findings or conclusions and do not monopolise the question and discussion time. Make a note of helpful comments to follow up later. Learn from watching good presenters and ask them for tips.

Teaching

It is advisable to start a teaching career at a level below the one you have just qualified for, or your confidence may suffer and your anxiety may escalate. It is probably important to have gained experience of teaching, tutoring and examining before applying for posts as course tutors. However, there are other ways you can gain experience, such as being a supervisor, personal therapist for trainees, visiting lecturer, personal development group leader, research adviser, and so on.

Running short courses is another way that you can develop your professional portfolio of experience, and often this is best started by joining a group of associate trainers. Some organisations that provide free counselling services also provide training and put on short courses for their trainees and associates. Learning the whole process of course development, marketing, finance, premises, administration and managing the day could be useful if you plan to develop this side of your professional work.